HOW WE LIVED

TRIBES AND EMPIRES

Series Editor: Dr. John Haywood

southwater

This edition is published by Southwater

Southwater is an imprint of Anness Publishing Ltd
Hermes House, 88–89 Blackfriars Road, London SE1 8HA
tel. 020 7401 2077; fax 020 7633 9499
www.southwaterbooks.com; info@anness.com

© Anness Publishing Ltd 2001, 2003

UK agent: The Manning Partnership Ltd,
6 The Old Dairy, Melcombe Road, Bath BA2 3LR;
tel. 01225 478444; fax 01225 478440;
sales@manning-partnership.co.uk

UK distributor: Grantham Book Services Ltd,
Isaac Newton Way, Alma Park Industrial Estate,
Grantham, Lincs NG31 9SD;
tel. 01476 541080; fax 01476 541061;
orders@gbs.tbs-ltd.co.uk

North American agent/distributor: National Book Network,
4501 Forbes Boulevard, Suite 200, Lanham, MD 20706;
tel. 301 459 3366; fax 301 429 5746; www.nbnbooks.com

Australian agent/distributor: Pan Macmillan Australia,
Level 18, St Martins Tower, 31 Market St, Sydney, NSW 2000;
tel. 1300 135 113; fax 1300 135 103;
customer.service@macmillan.com.au

New Zealand agent/distributor: David Bateman Ltd,
30 Tarndale Grove, Off Bush Road, Albany, Auckland;
tel. (09) 415 7664; fax (09) 415 8892

Publisher: Joanna Lorenz
Managing Editor, Children's Books: Gilly Cameron Cooper
Project Editors: Rasha Elsaeed, Rebecca Clunes
Assistant Editor: Sarah Uttridge
Editorial Reader: Joy Wotton
Introduction: Gilly Cameron Cooper
Authors: Daud Ali, Charlotte Hurdman, Fiona Macdonald,
Lorna Oakes, Philip Steele, Richard Tames, Michael Stotter
Consultants: Nick Allen, Clara Bezanilla, Felicity Cobbing,
Jenny Hall, Dr John Haywood, Dr Robin Holgate, Michael Johnson,
Jessie Lim, Louise Schofield and Leslie Webster
Designers: Simon Borrough, Matthew Cook, John Jamieson,
Caroline Reeves, Margaret Sadler, Alison Walker and
Stuart Watkinson at Ideas Into Print
Special Photography: John Freeman
Stylists: Konica Shankar, Thomasina Smith and Melanie Williams
Illustrations: Rob Ashby, Julian Baker, Vaness Card, Stuart Carter,
Chris Forsey, Shane Marsh, Rob Sheffield and Clive Spong,
Shane Watson
Production Controller: Claire Rae

PICTURE CREDITS
b=bottom, t=top, c=center, l=left, r=right

AKG: 8tl, 12tl, 13cr, 25tr, 60r; Lesley and Roy Adkins: 39cr;
Ancient Art and Architecture Collection: 14b, 19tc, 21ct, 33tr,
36cr, 37br, 42b, 42l, 43tl, 43tc, 44cl, 49tr, 49cr; Bildarchiv
Preussischer Kulturbesitz: 13tr; Bridgeman Art Library: 20tr, 21tl,
33cr, 55tl; British Museum: 48tr; Corbis: 20cl, 56, 57br; James
Davis: 27tr, 54br; C.M Dixon: 18tr, 18b, 19b, 24tl, 32c, 36c, 37tr,
37cl, 57tl, 57tc, 57tr; E.T Archive: 25c, 30l, 31tl, 31tr, 31bl, 55br;
Mary Evans: 36tl, 37tl, 43bl, 43br; Robert Harding: 9t; Michael
Holford: 9cr, 12tr, 13tl, 26tl, 39tr, 51c; Griffith Institute,
Ashmolean Museum: 14t; Link Photo Library: 21c; Macquitty
Collection: 27c; Peter Newark: 60tl, 60tr, 61tl, 61tc; Ann and Bury
Peerless: 25tl; Pierpont Morgan Library/Art source, New York:
45cr; Planet Earth Pictures Ltd: 39b; South American Photo Library:
50br, 51tl, 54tl, 55tl; Tony Stone: 38–39; University of Oslo: 48cr;
Visual Arts Library: 30r, 31br; Werner Forman Archive 50tl; Zefa:
15r, 18tl, 19tl, 19tr, 26c, 42r

Previously published as
Tribes, Empires and Civilizations Through The Ages

10 9 8 7 6 5 4 3 2 1

CONTENTS

KEY

Look out for the border patterns used throughout this book. They will help you identify each culture.

Mesopotamia	Chinese Empire	The Vikings
Ancient Egypt	Ancient Greece	Mesoamerica
Ancient India	Roman Empire	North Americans

A World of Difference

The members of a Stone Age community go about their everyday life. Groups of families joined forces so that they could protect themselves better. They could also pool their resources and skills to hunt more successfully and improve their way of life. Several communities like this might be part of a tribal culture that shared a similar language, beliefs, traditions and way of living.

Today, we know a lot about people who live in different countries all over the world. We see them on television and read about them in books. But for many groups of people in the past, their tribe was their world. Everyone knew everyone else within the community. The earliest groups probably had no idea of the true extent of the world and what everyday life was like for people outside their tribe.

Tribal people develop a particular way of doing things – of dressing, cooking and living, of traditions and crafts – based on the raw materials they have. If there is no need for change, or no ideas come from outside to inspire change, tribal societies often continue living in the same way, with the same language and traditions, for centuries.

There's a world of difference in a civilized society. People no longer travel from place to place to hunt for food, as the early tribal societies did, but settle in villages, towns and cities. There are more people, with many different occupations and activities. They have more wealth and an endless catalog of needs – for homes and other buildings, goods and services, roads and transportation. Law and social organization became necessary to help things run smoothly and

Early settlements grew up near rivers, lakes or the ocean. The land had to be fertile to grow crops for food. Fish was a good alternative source of food, and water provided transportation as well as irrigation for crops. These communities were the first step toward civilization.

The hanging gardens of Babylon were King Nebuchadnezzar's gift to his wife. They were to make her feel more at home in the desert, as she came from a country of green hills. One mark of a civilization is an upper class with plenty of wealth to spend. Rulers usually liked to create something by which they would be remembered for eternity, such as splendid temples and palaces.

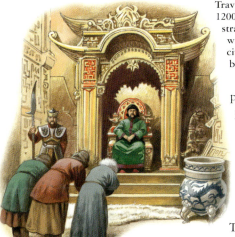

Travelers from the West are received at court in China. During the 1200s, they carried stories of splendid palaces, fabulous wealth and strange customs back to Europe. China was cut off from the rest of the world by mountains, deserts and ocean, and built up its own unique civilization. The Chinese progressed in many areas of technology long before the West, and had quite different ways of behaving.

people to live together peacefully. Life in a civilized society is very complicated – this is what makes it so different from tribal life. Solving the problems of such large and complicated communities is a constant spur to human ingenuity and inventiveness. New inventions and ways of making life easier are tested out all the time, and the pace of progress and change is fast.

The people of the very first civilizations, such as Mesopotamia and Egypt, had to learn how to solve these problems for themselves. No one else had ever had to face them before. Later civilizations, such as Rome, learned from the older ones as new ideas came in from the outside – from traders, travelers and soldiers. Civilizations became exciting melting pots of many different peoples, ideas and lifestyles.

In every civilization and culture, there are rulers, thinkers and inventors who have shaped the course of history. King Ashurbanipal (669–631 BC) contributed the world's first library to civilization. He was also a ruthless empire-builder. Throughout history, there have been leaders like him, who have wanted to increase their power and conquer other lands. They forced the conquered countries to give them a share of their wealth and resources. Some empire-builders, such as Alexander the Great, allowed conquered nations to keep their national identities. Others, such as the Spanish in Mesoamerica, wiped out the native religion, language, laws and lifestyle almost completely.

The world is very different today. There are fewer subject peoples and no great empires. Countries have their own national identities, but may be made up of many different races and tribes, religions and ways of life. This book presents some of the building blocks of today's world.

The Romans marked the northern limit of their empire in England by building Hadrian's Wall from coast to coast. Beyond it lived the barbarians! It was hard work and very expensive for an empire to keep control of the territories it had won.

Life in the Stone Age

THE STONE AGE is the longest period of human history. It began two million years ago, when the ancestors of modern humans started to use stone tools. Gradually, using their tools and their intelligence, they learned how to adapt to different environments. Humans began to move out of Africa, where they had first evolved, and by 10,000BC they had settled on every continent except Antarctica. The Stone Age came to an end when people began to work metals on a large scale.

Stone Age people lived in groups called clans, that were made up of several families, probably closely related to each other. It was safer to live in a clan than as a single family unit, and groups of people could work as a team when hunting or gathering food. As generations passed, the clans grew into bigger, tribal communities. Close family relationships diluted through the generations, but everyone shared the same ancestor. Some communities grew bigger still and split into different tribes that moved to other areas. They kept the same language, beliefs and traditions – they were still part of the same tribal culture. In some tribal cultures, different tribes gathered at certain times of the year, for festivals or meetings. Their lifestyle remained much the same for the rest of the year, though, as hunter-gatherers or simple farmers.

mastodon, Canada
20,000BC

bison,
North America
9000BC

NORTH AMERIC

CENTRAL AME

agriculture, South America
7000BC

Origins of agriculture

cave art, Argent.
8500BC

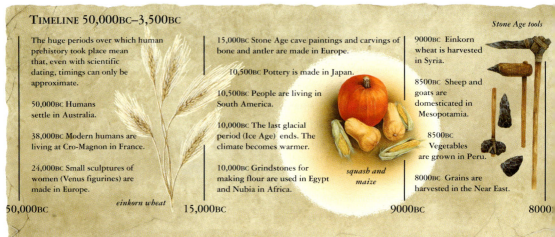

TIMELINE 50,000BC–3,500BC

Stone Age tools

The huge periods over which human prehistory took place mean that, even with scientific dating, timings can only be approximate.

50,000BC Humans settle in Australia.

38,000BC Modern humans are living at Cro-Magnon in France.

24,000BC Small sculptures of women (Venus figurines) are made in Europe.

einkorn wheat

15,000BC Stone Age cave paintings and carvings of bone and antler are made in Europe.

10,500BC Pottery is made in Japan.

10,500BC People are living in South America.

10,000BC The last glacial period (Ice Age) ends. The climate becomes warmer.

10,000BC Grindstones for making flour are used in Egypt and Nubia in Africa.

squash and maize

9000BC Einkorn wheat is harvested in Syria.

8500BC Sheep and goats are domesticated in Mesopotamia.

8500BC Vegetables are grown in Peru.

8000BC Grains are harvested in the Near East.

50,000BC   15,000BC   9000BC   8000

migrating reindeer, Russia
15,000BC

EUROPE

clay figurine,
Czech Republic
24,000BC

ASIA

cave art, France
15,000BC

pottery, Japan
10,500BC

settlement,
Turkey
6,500BC

rock art,
Sahara
6000BC

Peking Man, China
460,0000BC

Homo erectus *skull*,
Java, 120,000BC

AFRICA

Homo habilis *skull, Kenya
2.5 million years ago*

cave art, Namibia
8000BC

AUSTRALIA

SOUTH AMERICA

N

indigenous peoples,
Australia
50,000BC

THE STONE AGE WORLD
This map shows places of
importance during the Stone Age.

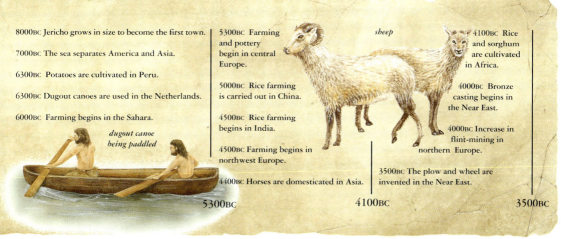

8000BC Jericho grows in size to become the first town.

7000BC The sea separates America and Asia.

6300BC Potatoes are cultivated in Peru.

6300BC Dugout canoes are used in the Netherlands.

6000BC Farming begins in the Sahara.

*dugout canoe
being paddled*

5300BC Farming
and pottery
begin in central
Europe.

5000BC Rice farming
is carried out in China.

4500BC Rice farming
begins in India.

4500BC Farming begins in
northwest Europe.

4400BC Horses are domesticated in Asia.

sheep

4100BC Rice
and sorghum
are cultivated
in Africa.

4000BC Bronze
casting begins in
the Near East.

4000BC Increase in
flint-mining in
northern Europe.

3500BC The plow and wheel are
invented in the Near East.

5300BC

4100BC

3500BC

Mesopotamia's First Empires

Mesopotamia is the name of an ancient region where some of the world's first cities and empires grew up. Mesopotamia means "the land between the rivers" – for the country lay between the Tigris and the Euphrates, two mighty rivers that flowed from the highlands of Turkey in the north down to the Gulf. Today, most of it lies in modern Iraq.

The first farmers settled in the low, rolling hills of the north about 9,000 years ago. Here, there was enough rainfall to grow crops and provide pasture for animals. The land in north Mesopotamia became known as Assyria.

The first cities developed about 3,500 years later, mostly in the fertile plains of the south. This area had rivers and marshes which provided water to irrigate crops and reeds to build houses and boats. Fish, dates and other food were easy to find. At first the south was called Sumer. Later it was known as Babylonia.

SUMERIAN WORSHIPPERS
Statues of a man and woman from Sumer are shown in an act of worship. The Sumerians were some of the earliest people to live in the south of Mesopotamia. They lived in small, independent cities. At the center of each city was a temple built as the home for the local god. These two Sumerians had statues made of themselves and put in a temple, so that the god could bless them.

THE WORK OF GIANTS
Most of what we know about the ancient civilizations of Mesopotamia has come from excavations by archaeologists over the last 150 years. In 1845, the British archaeologist Henry Layard unearthed the remains of a once-magnificent palace in the ancient Assyrian city of Nimrud. He found walls decorated with scenes of battles and hunting, and a statue of a human-headed, winged lion so huge that local people were astonished and thought it had been made by giants.

TIMELINE 7000BC–2100BC

Humans have lived in northern Iraq since the Old Stone Age, when hunter-gatherers lived in caves and rock shelters and made stone tools. Mesopotamian civilization began when people began to settle in villages. They learned how to grow crops and keep animals. Later, city-states grew up, and people developed writing. They became good at building, working metal and making fine jewelry.

painted pottery

7000BC The first villages are established. Edible plants and animals are domesticated, and farming develops. Pottery is made and mud bricks used for building.

6000BC Use of copper. First mural paintings, temples and seals. Irrigation is used in agriculture to bring water to the fields. Decorated pottery, clay and alabaster figurines. Wide use of brick.

clay figurine

4000BC Larger houses and temples are built. Terra-cotta sickles and pestles are developed.

3500BC Growth of towns. Development of the potter's wheel, the plow, the first cylinder seals and writing. Bronze, silver and gold worked. Sculptures are made. Trading systems develop.

writing tablet

3000BC Sumerian civilization begins. City-states and writing develop.

7000BC   4000BC   2700B

TEMPLES OF THE GODS

The ziggurat of Nanna, the Moon god, rises above the dusty plains of modern Iraq. It was once part of the massive temple complex in the city of Ur. Ziggurats show how clever the Mesopotamians were at building. They were designed as a link between heaven and earth.

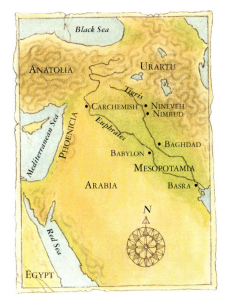

WRITING TABLET

A clay tablet shows an example of some of the earliest writing in the world. The symbols were pressed into a damp clay tablet using a reed pen. The Sumerians originally used writing to keep accounts of goods bought and sold, including grain and cattle. Later on, kings used clay tablets as a record of their victories and building activities. Scribes wrote letters, poems and stories about heroes.

POWERFUL NEIGHBORS

By about 2000BC the Assyrians were trading with Anatolia in the north-west of Mesopotamia. The Assyrians later conquered Phoenician cities in the west and fought Urartu in the north.

Sumerian chariot

2700BC Early Dynastic period. Kings and city administrations rule.

2600BC Royal Standard of Ur made, probably as the sounding box of a lyre.

2500BC Royal Graves of Ur made. Queen Pu-abi and other wealthy individuals buried in tombs with soldiers, musicians and court ladies.

2440BC Interstate warfare. Kings of Lagash go to war with Umma.

2334BC Sargon of Agade becomes king. He creates the world's first empire, which is maintained by his grandson Naram-sin.

Pu-abi

2200BC The Agade Empire comes to an end. The Gutians, a mountain people, move into Mesopotamia and take some cities.

ziggurat of Ur-nammu

2141BC Gudea takes the throne of Lagash. Ambitious temple-building program at Girsu.

2112BC Ur-nammu of Ur tries to re-create the Agade Empire. He builds the famous ziggurat of Ur.

2500BC   2200BC   2100BC

City-states of Mesopotamia

MANY OF THE GREAT EMPIRES in Mesopotamia grew up around small city-states. Each state consisted of a city and the surrounding countryside, and had its own ruler and god. Uruk, in the south, was the first state to become important, in 2,700BC. Its leader was called Gilgamesh and many legends grew up around him.

Around 2300BC, a leader called Sargon conquered all the cities of Mesopotamia and several in neighboring lands. In doing so, he created the world's first empire. After his dynasty died out in about 2150BC, the kings of Ur, a city further south, tried to re-create Sargon's empire, but with limited success. Ur fell to the Elamites, invaders from a region in the east. About 100 years later, a nomadic people called the Amorites settled in Mesopotamia. They took over the old Sumerian cities, including Babylon, and several of their chiefs became kings.

Meanwhile, in the north, the Assyrian Empire had grown from its beginnings in the city-state of Ashur. It developed slowly over 2,000 years and reached a glorious peak around 645BC. The Empire crumbled when the Babylonians conquered their key cities in 612BC. Babylonia became the most powerful empire in the known world until it was conquered by the Persian king, Cyrus, in 539BC.

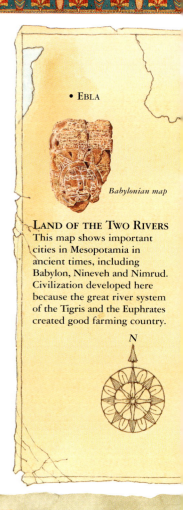

• EBLA

Babylonian map

LAND OF THE TWO RIVERS
This map shows important cities in Mesopotamia in ancient times, including Babylon, Nineveh and Nimrud. Civilization developed here because the great river system of the Tigris and the Euphrates created good farming country.

N

TIMELINE 2100BC–1000BC

2004BC Ibbi-Sin, last king of Ur, is captured by Elamites and taken to Susa.

2000BC Fall of the Sumerian Empire. Amorites interrupt trade routes. Ur attacked by Elamites and falls. Assyria becomes independent and establishes trading network in Anatolia.

1900BC Amorite chiefs take over some cities as rulers.

1792BC Hammurabi, an Amorite ruler, becomes King of Babylon.

Hammurabi

1787BC King Hammurabi conquers the major southern city of Isin.

1763BC Hammurabi conquers the city of Larsa.

1761BC Hammurabi conquers Mari and Eshnunna and may have conquered the city of Ashur.

1740BC Expansion of the Hittite kingdom in Anatolia, based on the city of Hattusas.

scorpion man

1595BC The Hittite king, Mursulis, conquers North Syria. Marching further south, he destroys Babylon but does not take over the city.

1570BC The Kassites, a foreign dynasty, begin a 400-year rule of peace and prosperity. King Kurigalzu builds a new capital city, naming it after himself. Babylon becomes a world power on an equal level with the kingdom of Egypt.

2100BC   1790BC   1600BC   1500B[C]

Lake Urmia

Greater Zab

• NINEVEH

NIMRUD •

ASSYRIA

royal chariot

lion hunting

ASHUR •

Lesser Zab

eagle-headed god

Khabur

MARI •

Euphrates

duck weight

Tigris

Diyala

winged bull

lyre

lion-headed eagle

• SIPPAR

ELAM

Kark-heh

• KISH

• BABYLON

SUSA •

archer

code of Hammurabi

BABYLONIA

• NIPPUR

UMMA •

• GIRSU

URUK •

• LAGASH

Royal Standard of Ur

SUMER

UR •

Karun

ziggurat at Ur

TELL AL'-UBAID •

• ERIDU

date palms

The Gulf

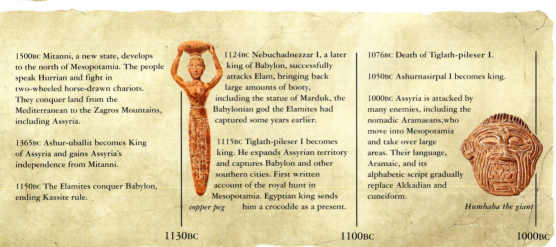

1500BC Mitanni, a new state, develops to the north of Mesopotamia. The people speak Hurrian and fight in two-wheeled horse-drawn chariots. They conquer land from the Mediterranean to the Zagros Mountains, including Assyria.

1365BC Ashur-uballit becomes King of Assyria and gains Assyria's independence from Mitanni.

1150BC The Elamites conquer Babylon, ending Kassite rule.

1124BC Nebuchadnezzar I, a later king of Babylon, successfully attacks Elam, bringing back large amounts of booty, including the statue of Marduk, the Babylonian god the Elamites had captured some years earlier.

1115BC Tiglath-pileser I becomes king. He expands Assyrian territory and captures Babylon and other southern cities. First written account of the royal hunt in Mesopotamia. Egyptian king sends him a crocodile as a present.

copper peg

1076BC Death of Tiglath-pileser I.

1050BC Ashurnasirpal I becomes king.

1000BC Assyria is attacked by many enemies, including the nomadic Aramaeans, who move into Mesopotamia and take over large areas. Their language, Aramaic, and its alphabetic script gradually replace Akkadian and cuneiform.

Humbaba the giant

1130BC

1100BC

1000BC

Mesopotamian Leader

Tʜᴇ ɴᴀᴍᴇs ᴏꜰ Mesopotamian kings are known because their victories and other achievements were recorded on clay tablets and palace wall decorations. The kings wanted to be sure that the gods knew that they had ruled well, and that their names would be remembered forever. The names of ordinary soldiers and temple builders, the craftsmen who created the beautiful painted wall reliefs and the authors of the sagas and histories were not written down. Some astrologers, army commanders and state officials are known by name because they wrote letters to the king.

EANNATUM OF LAGASH (C. 2440BC)
Eannatum was king of Lagash, a city in southern Sumer. He was a great warrior and temple-builder. His victory over the nearby state of Umma was recorded on the Vulture Stela, a limestone carving that showed vultures pecking at the bodies of dead soldiers.

SARGON OF AGADE (2334–2279BC)
King Sargon created the world's first empire by conquering all the cities of Sumer, Mari and Ebla. He founded the city of Agade, no trace of which has yet been found. A legend says that when Sargon was a baby, his mother put him in a reed basket and set him afloat on a river. The man who found him trained him to be a gardener. When Sargon grew up, it was believed that he had been favored by the goddess Ishtar, and he became cup-bearer to the king of Kish (a city north of Babylon).

ENHEDUANNA(C. 2250BC)
The daughter of King Sargon of Agade is one of the few women in Mesopotamian history whose name is known. She held the important post of high priestess to the Moon-god at Ur. Her hymn to the god made her the first known woman author.

TIMELINE 1000BC–500BC

stela of Ashurnasirpal II

black obelisk of Shalmaneser III

Balawat Gates

911ʙᴄ Adad-nirari becomes king. Assyria recovers some of her lost possessions and defeats the Aramaeans and Babylon.

879ʙᴄ Ashurnasirpal II holds a banquet to celebrate the opening of his new palace at Nimrud.

858ʙᴄ Shalmaneser III, son of Ashurnasirpal II, spends most of his 34-year reign at war, campaigning in Syria, Phoenicia, Urartu and the Zagros Mountains.

c. 845ʙᴄ Palace of Balawat built.

744ʙᴄ Tiglath-pileser III brings more territory under direct Assyrian control. Deportation of conquered peoples begins.

721ʙᴄ Sargon II decorates his palace at Khorsabad with carved reliefs showing his battle victories.

705ʙᴄ Sennacherib becomes king of Assyria.

701ʙᴄ Sennacherib attacks Hezekiah in Jerusalem.

694ʙᴄ Ashur-nadin-shumi rules Babylon on behalf of his father Sennacherib. He is captured by the Elamites and taken to Susa. In revenge, Sennacherib burns Babylon to the ground.

1000ʙᴄ   850ʙᴄ   710ʙᴄ   690ʙᴄ

HAMMURABI (1792–1750

King Hammurabi of Babylo
collected 282 laws concerning
family, town and business life
and had them recorded on a
black stela, a large stone.
Other rulers had made
laws, but his is the largest
collection to survive.
The picture shows
Shamash, god of justice,
giving Hammurabi the
symbols of kingship.
Toward the end of his
reign, he went to war
and created an empire,
but it did not last long
after his death.

ASHURBANIPAL OF ASSYRIA (669–631 BC)

A great warrior king, Ashurbanipal reigned at
the peak of the Assyrian Empire. He fought
successfully against the Elamites, Babylonians
and Arabs, and even made Egypt part of his
empire for a time. However, his greatest gift to
civilization was the vast library in his palaces at
Nineveh. Here, over 25,000 clay tablets were
collected, including letters, legends and
astronomical, mathematical and medical works.

NEBUCHADNEZZAR II (604–562BC)

As crown prince, Nebuchadnezzar fought at the side
of his father, the king of Babylon, and brought the
Assyrian Empire to an end. Under his own rule,
the Babylonians conquered neighboring countries,
such as Palestine, and became one of the world
powers of the time. Nebuchadnezzar built great
fortifying walls around the city of Babylon and a
magnificent ziggurat. He features in the Bible, as
the king who captured Jerusalem and sent the
people of Judah into captivity.

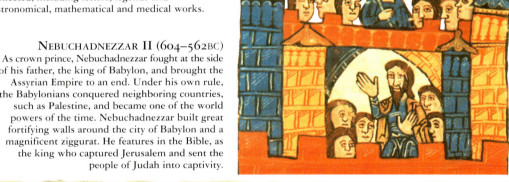

681BC Sennacherib killed by his
eldest son. His youngest son
Esarhaddon becomes king.

671BC Esarhaddon invades
Egypt and captures the Egyptian
capital of Memphis.

668BC Ashurbanipal becomes
king of Assyria. His
brother Shamash-shum-
ukin becomes king of Babylon.

Tiglath-pileser III

664BC Ashurbanipal invades Egypt and
destroys the southern city of Thebes.

663 or 653BC Ashurbanipal begins a series
of wars with Elam.

652BC Rebellion of Shamash-shum-ukin.
Ashurbanipal invades Babylonia.

648BC Ashurbanipal lays siege to Babylon,
which suffers starvation.

631BC Death of
Ashurbanipal.
Assyrian Empire
begins to
collapse.

Nimrud

612BC Babylonians attack and
burn the Assyrian cities of
Nimrud and Nineveh.

605BC Assyrians
defeated by the
Babylonians at the
battle of Carchemish.

*Ashurbanipal on
horseback*

604BC Nebuchadnezzar II becomes King of
Babylon, and Babylon becomes a world power.

562BC Nebuchadnezzar II dies.

539BC Cyrus of Persia takes Babylon.

663BC   620BC   500BC

Egyptian Civilization

HORUS' EYE
This symbol can be seen on many Egyptian artefacts. It is the eye of the god Horus.

E GYPT IS A COUNTRY at the crossroads of Africa, Europe and Asia. If you could step back in time 5,000 years, you would discover an amazing civilization – the kingdom of the ancient Egyptians.

Most of Egypt is made up of baking hot, sandy deserts. These are crossed by the river Nile as it snakes its way north to the Mediterranean Sea. Every year, floods cover the banks of the Nile with mud. Plants grow well in this rich soil, and 8,000 years ago farmers were planting crops here. Wealth from farming led to trade and to the building of towns. By 3100BC a great kingdom had grown up in Egypt, ruled by royal families.

Ancient Egypt existed for over 3,000 years. Pyramids, temples and artefacts survive from this period to show us what life was like in the land of the pharaohs.

AMAZING DISCOVERIES
In 1922, the English archaeologist Howard Carter made an amazing discovery. He found the tomb of the young pharaoh Tutankhamun. No single find in Egypt has ever provided as much evidence as the discovery of this well-preserved tomb.

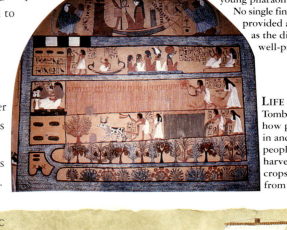

LIFE BY THE NILE
Tomb paintings show us how people lived in ancient Egypt. Here people water and harvest their crops, using water from the river Nile.

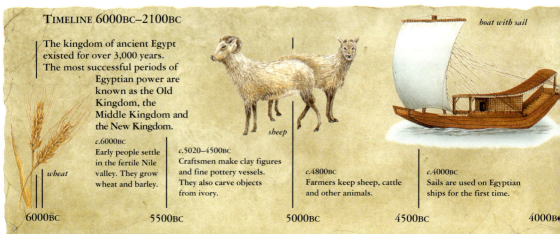

TIMELINE 6000BC–2100BC

boat with sail

The kingdom of ancient Egypt existed for over 3,000 years. The most successful periods of Egyptian power are known as the Old Kingdom, the Middle Kingdom and the New Kingdom.

wheat

sheep

c.6000BC
Early people settle in the fertile Nile valley. They grow wheat and barley.

c.5020–4500BC
Craftsmen make clay figures and fine pottery vessels. They also carve objects from ivory.

c.4800BC
Farmers keep sheep, cattle and other animals.

c.4000BC
Sails are used on Egyptian ships for the first time.

6000BC	5500BC	5000BC	4500BC	4000B•

THE KINGDOM OF EGYPT

This map of Egypt today shows where there were important cities and sites in ancient times. The ancient Egyptians lived mostly along the banks of the river Nile and in the green, fertile lands of the delta. Through the ages, the Egyptians built many imposing temples in honour of their gods and mysterious tombs to house their dead. Most of these temples and tombs were built close to the major cities of Memphis and Thebes.

Map labels:

Rosetta (el-Rashid)
Alexandria
Nile delta
Giza
Saqqara
Memphis
LOWER EGYPT
Dahshur
Maidum
Sinai
Beni-Hasan
Akhetaten (el-Amarna)
River Nile
UPPER EGYPT
Abydos
Valley of the Kings
Karnak
Thebes (Luxor)
Kharga Oasis
Aswan
Philae

△ Pyramid
⚲ Valley of the Kings
⚱ Ancient Site

Abu Simbel

SURVIVORS OF THE DESERT

The face of the great pharaoh Ramesses II stares out at us. Huge statues of Ramesses were part of a temple cut from the rock face at Abu Simbel in 1269BC. During the 1960s the statues had to be raised because a new dam at Aswan turned this part of the Nile into a lake. Temples, tombs and statues such as those at Abu Simbel have survived for thousands of years in the dry desert heat. More recently, many monuments have started to disintegrate because of the polluted air around modern cities such as Luxor.

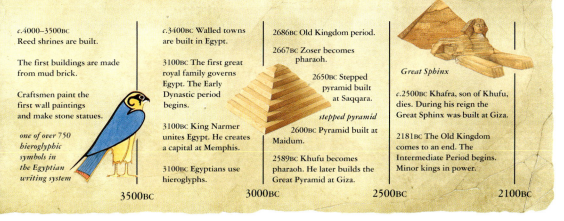

c.4000–3500BC Reed shrines are built.

The first buildings are made from mud brick.

Craftsmen paint the first wall paintings and make stone statues.

one of over 750 hieroglyphic symbols in the Egyptian writing system

c.3400BC Walled towns are built in Egypt.

3100BC The first great royal family governs Egypt. The Early Dynastic period begins.

3100BC King Narmer unites Egypt. He creates a capital at Memphis.

3100BC Egyptians use hieroglyphs.

2686BC Old Kingdom period.

2667BC Zoser becomes pharaoh.

2650BC Stepped pyramid built at Saqqara.

stepped pyramid

2600BC Pyramid built at Maidum.

2589BC Khufu becomes pharaoh. He later builds the Great Pyramid at Giza.

Great Sphinx

c.2500BC Khafra, son of Khufu, dies. During his reign the Great Sphinx was built at Giza.

2181BC The Old Kingdom comes to an end. The Intermediate Period begins. Minor kings in power.

3500BC   3000BC   2500BC   2100BC

The Kingdom on the Nile

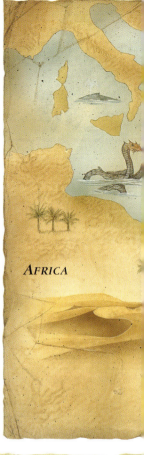

THE STORY OF ANCIENT EGYPT began about 8,000 years ago when farmers started to plant crops and raise animals in the Nile Valley. By about 3400BC the Egyptians were building walled towns. Soon after that the northern part of the country (Lower Egypt) was united with the lands upstream (Upper Egypt) to form one country under a single king. The capital of this new kingdom was established at Memphis.

The first great period of Egyptian civilization is called the Old Kingdom. It lasted from 2686BC to 2181BC. This was when the pharaohs built great pyramids, the massive tombs that still stand in the desert today.

During the Middle Kingdom (2050–1786BC), the capital was moved south, to the city of Thebes. The Egyptians gained control of Nubia and extended the area of land being farmed. Despite this period of success, the rule of the royal families of ancient Egypt was sometimes interrupted by disorder. In 1663BC, control of the country fell into foreign hands. The Hyksos, a group of Asian settlers, ruled Egypt for almost 100 years.

In 1567BC the Hyksos were overthrown by the princes of Thebes. The Thebans established the New Kingdom. This was the highest point of Egyptian civilization. Traders and soldiers traveled into Africa, Asia and the lands of the Mediterranean. However, by 525BC, the might of the Egyptians was coming to an end and Egypt became part of the Persian Empire. In 332BC rule passed to the Greeks. Finally, in 30BC, conquest was complete as Egypt fell under the control of the Roman Empire.

AFRICA

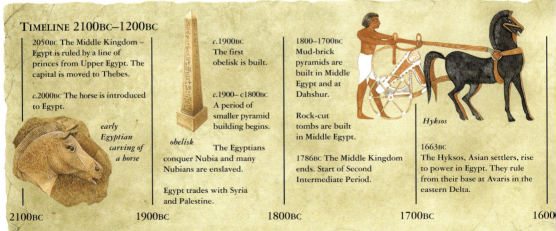

TIMELINE 2100BC–1200BC

2050BC The Middle Kingdom – Egypt is ruled by a line of princes from Upper Egypt. The capital is moved to Thebes.

c.2000BC The horse is introduced to Egypt.

early Egyptian carving of a horse

obelisk

c.1900BC The first obelisk is built.

c.1900– c1800BC A period of smaller pyramid building begins.

The Egyptians conquer Nubia and many Nubians are enslaved.

Egypt trades with Syria and Palestine.

1800–1700BC Mud-brick pyramids are built in Middle Egypt and at Dahshur.

Rock-cut tombs are built in Middle Egypt.

1786BC The Middle Kingdom ends. Start of Second Intermediate Period.

Hyksos

1663BC The Hyksos, Asian settlers, rise to power in Egypt. They rule from their base at Avaris in the eastern Delta.

2100BC   1900BC   1800BC   1700BC   1600

EUROPE

Kadesh battle site

...naean Empire

Hittite Empire

MINOAN CRETE

Byblos.

Mediterranean Sea

LEVANT

Megiddo.

Jerusalem .

. Avaris

SYRIA

PALESTINE

MESOPOTAMIA

North

ASIA

LOWER EGYPT

. Memphis Sinai

River Nile

EGYPT

Western Desert

Thebes .

UPPER EGYPT

ARABIA

NUBIA

Red Sea

MAP OF THE NEAR EAST

In 1279BC, at the height of
the New Kingdom,
Egypt was a leading
power in the Near East.
The country was prosperous
and rich, trading with Minoan Crete,
Syria, the Levant and Nubia.
Nevertheless, it faced threats from
enemies such as the Hittites.

Akhenaten

c1567BC The Hyksos are
defeated by Egyptians from the
southern city of Thebes.

1550BC The New Kingdom
is founded. Royal
tombs are built in the
Valley of the Kings.

1525BC Amenhotep
becomes pharaoh.

1500BC A village is
founded at Deir el-
Medina, near the
Valley of the Kings.

Thutmose III

1498BC Queen Hatshepsut
rules as co-regent with the
child king Thutmose III.

1483BC Hatshepsut dies.

1478BC The rebellious
prince of Kadesh is
defeated by
Thutmose III at the
Battle of Megiddo
in the Near East.
*the cartouche of
Tutankhamun*

1379BC
Akhenaten
introduces
worship of the
Sun god, Aten, as
the only religion.
A new capital is
established at el-Amarna.

c1334BC Smenkhkare,
Akhenaten's successor, moves
the capital back to Memphis.

1325BC Tutankhamun is
buried in the Valley of
the Kings.

1291BC Seti I comes to power.
He builds the Hypostyle Hall
at Karnak.

1279BC
Ramesses
II becomes
pharaoh.

Ramesses II

1274BC Ramesses II fights
the Hittites at the battle
of Kadesh.

1500BC   1400BC   1300BC   1200BC

Famous Pharaohs

KHAFRA
(reigned 2558–2532BC)
Khafra is the son of the pharaoh Khufu. He is remembered for his splendid tomb, the Second Pyramid at Giza and the Great Sphinx that guards it.

AMENHOTEP I
(reigned 1525–1504BC)
The pharaoh Amenhotep led the Egyptian army to battle in Nubia. He also founded a village for workmen at Deir el-Medina.

FOR THOUSANDS OF YEARS ancient Egypt was ruled by royal families. We know much about the pharaohs (kings) and queens from these great dynasties because of their magnificent tombs and the public monuments raised in their honour.

Egypt's first ruler was King Narmer, who united the country in about 3100BC. Later pharaohs such as Zoser and Khufu are remembered for the great pyramids they had built as their tombs.

Pharaohs usually succeeded to the throne through royal birth. However, in some cases military commanders such as Horemheb came to power. Although Egypt's rulers were traditionally men, a few powerful women were made pharaoh. The most famous of these is the Greek queen Cleopatra, who ruled Egypt in 51BC.

HATSHEPSUT
(reigned 1498–1483BC)
Hatshepsut was the half-sister and wife of Thutmose II. When her husband died, she was appointed to rule Egypt until her young stepson Thutmose III was old enough. However Queen Hatshepsut was ambitious and had herself crowned pharaoh. Hatshepsut is famous for her trading expeditions to the land of Punt. The walls of her temple at Deir el-Bahri show these exotic trips.

TIMELINE 1200BC–AD1960

Ramesses III

1198BC Mediterranean Sea peoples attack Egypt.

1182BC Ramesses III, the last great warrior pharaoh, comes to power. He defeats the Mediterranean Sea peoples in battle.

1151BC The last great pharaoh, Ramesses III, dies.

c.1070BC The New Kingdom ends. Start of Third Intermediate Period.

900–700BC Brief periods of calm between conquest by invading armies.

671BC Assyrians conquer Egypt as far as Memphis.

Darius I

525BC Beginning of the Late Dynastic Period. Egypt becomes part of the Persian Empire.

332BC Egypt is invaded by Alexander the Great and is ruled by Greek kings. Alexandria is built.

305BC Ptolemy I, a commander in Alexander the Great's army, takes power after his death.

Alexander the Great

51BC Cleopatra VII, Ptolemy's XII's daughter, reigns in Egypt.

Cleopatra VII

30BC Egypt becomes part of the Roman Empire under the emperor Augustus.

| 1200BC | 900BC | 600BC | 300BC | AD0 |

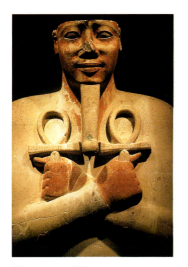

TUTANKHAMUN
(reigned 1334–1325BC)
This pharaoh came to the throne when he was only nine years old. He died at the age of 18. Tutankhamun is remembered for his tomb in the Valley of the Kings, which was packed with amazing treasures.

THUTMOSE III
(reigned 1479–1425BC)
Thutmose III is remembered as a brave warrior king. He launched many military campaigns against the Syrians in the Near East. Records from the time tell of Thutmose marching fearlessly into battle at the head of his army, unconcerned about his own safety. He won a famous victory at Megiddo and then later at Kadesh. Thutmose III was buried in the Valley of the Kings.

AKHENATEN
(reigned 1379–1334BC)
The Egyptians believed in many gods. However, when Akhenaten came to power, he introduced worship of one god, the Sun disk Aten. He moved the capital from Memphis to Akhetaten (now known as el-Amarna). His chief wife was the beautiful Queen Nefertiti.

RAMESSES II
(reigned 1279–1212BC)
One of the most famous pharaohs of all, Ramesses II, was the son of Seti I. He built many fine temples and defeated the Hittites at the Battle of Kadesh in 1274BC. The chief queen of Ramesses was Nefertari. Carvings of this graceful queen can be seen on Ramesses II's temple at Abu Simbel. Ramesses lived a long life and died at the age of 92. He was buried in the Valley of the Kings.

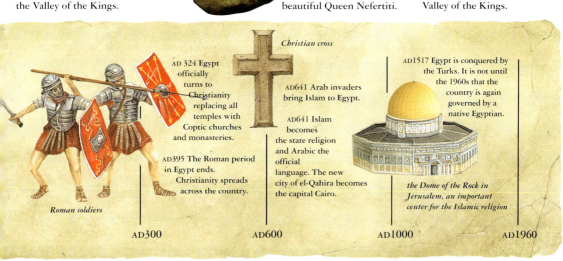

Christian cross

AD 324 Egypt officially turns to Christianity replacing all temples with Coptic churches and monasteries.

AD641 Arab invaders bring Islam to Egypt.

AD641 Islam becomes the state religion and Arabic the official language. The new city of el-Qahira becomes the capital Cairo.

AD1517 Egypt is conquered by the Turks. It is not until the 1960s that the country is again governed by a native Egyptian.

AD395 The Roman period in Egypt ends. Christianity spreads across the country.

the Dome of the Rock in Jerusalem, an important center for the Islamic religion

Roman soldiers

AD300   AD600   AD1000   AD1960

India's Glorious Heritage

THE INDIAN SUBCONTINENT IS HOME to one of the world's most varied civilizations because many different groups of people have traveled over the Himalayan mountains and settled there. From the arrival of Aryan tribes about 3,000 years ago until the invasion of the Moguls in the 1500s, each new wave of people brought fresh ideas and ways of life. As a result, India's religious and artistic life became very rich and mixed.

Two major world religions – Hinduism and Buddhism – developed in India, and for hundreds of years, India was also at the heart of Muslim life in Asia. These three religions shaped the course of India's history, and led to the building of magnificent monuments, many of which still stand.

With its Hindu and Buddhist temples and sculptures, and the sumptuous palaces of the Muslim rulers, India is full of amazing treasures from the past.

BEAUTY IN STONE
A beautiful carving of a Yakshi (tree spirit) from Bharhut in central India. It is made of red sandstone and dates from 100BC. This Buddhist sculpture has a distinctive Indian style that you can see in sculptures from much later periods. Buddhism was the first religion in India to inspire people to build monuments and make sculptures.

DAWN OF INDIAN CIVILIZATION
Ancient stone buildings, such as the Great Bath at Mohenjo-Daro in the Indus Valley, tell archaeologists a great deal about the dawn of civilization in India. Fewer buildings of later times have been excavated, partly because later houses were made of mud, thatch and wood, none of which has survived.

TIMELINE 6000BC–AD400

From early times until the coming of the British in 1757, India was divided into many kingdoms. It was never a single state. The regions of ancient India were linked by a common culture, rather than by politics, religion or language.

*c.*6000BC Neolithic settlements in Baluchistan.

*c.*2800–2600BC Beginnings of settlements in the Indus Valley region.

statue of priest king from Indus valley

rice cultivation

*c.*2300–1700BC The great cities of the Indus Valley (Mohenjo-Daro and Harappa), the Punjab (Kalibangan) and Gujarat (Lothal) flourished.

*c.*1700BC Sudden and mysterious decline of the Indus Valley civilization.

*c.*1500–1200BC Immigration of Vedic Aryans into north-western India.

*c.*1200–600BC The Vedic texts are composed.

*c.*800BC Use of iron for weapons and the spread of Aryan culture into the Gangetic plains (the area near the River Ganges).

*c.*500–300BC Rice cultivation and the introduction of iron agricultural tools in the eastern Gangetic plains lead to the formation of more complex societies, cities and states.

fragment of pot with brahmi inscription

6000BC	2500BC	1200BC	500BC

TEMPLE OF THE SUN
A huge carved stone wheel forms a panel on the wall of the Sun Temple at Konarak on India's east coast. This part of the temple is carved in the shape of a gigantic twelve-wheeled chariot, drawn by seven stone horses. It dates from the 1200s, when medieval Hindu kings built magnificent temples to their gods.

GRAND ENTRANCE
The Alamgiri Gate is one of three magnificent entrances built by the Mogul emperor Aurangzeb to the Shahadra fort at Lahore (in modern-day Pakistan). The fort doubled as a luxurious palace.

LIFE STORY
A limestone frieze from AD100 shows a good deed carried out by the spiritual leader known as the Buddha. The frieze comes from Amaravati, in southeastern India, an important Buddhist site from 300BC. Stories of the Buddha's past lives, called jatakas, were popular in ancient India.

A COUNTRY OF MOUNTAINS AND PLAINS
India is bounded to the north by the Himalayan mountains. The central Deccan plateau is framed by mountain ranges known as the Eastern and Western Ghats. The first settlements grew up near rivers on the fertile plains in the north.

c.500–400BC Inscribed fragments of pots from Sri Lanka discovered.

c.478–400BC Life of the Buddha. He is born a prince but leaves his family and lives in poverty.

327–325BC Alexander the Great arrives in northwestern India.

320BC The rise of the Magadhan Empire under the Maurya family, founded by King Chandragupta I.

coin of Alexander the Great

268–233BC King Ashoka, the grandson of Chandragupta I, issues the first royal edicts on pillars and rocks throughout the subcontinent.

c. 50BC–AD100 Intensive trade connections with the Roman Empire.

AD50–AD200 Kushanas and Shakas (tribes from Central Asia) set up kingdoms and adopt Indian religions. Indian dynasty of Satavahanas arises in southern India.

Ashokan pillar

c. AD150 Kushana and Shaka kings in the north and west adopt Sanskrit as the courtly language.

c. AD200–400 *Ramayana*, *Mahabharata* and the *Bhagavad-Gita* Hindu epic poems are composed in their final form.

AD400 Nearly all courts are using Sanskrit.

gateway to Buddhist stupa

300BC   AD100   AD400

The Land of Ancient India

INDIA IS ISOLATED FROM THE main continent of Asia by the world's highest mountains, the Himalayas. The mountains made it difficult for people to invade. The easiest overland route, taken by the earliest settlers from Asia, is from the northwest (present-day Afghanistan) through the Karakoram mountains. However, it was still a difficult journey. Once people had arrived in India, they tended to stay.

The first people settled in the bare mountain foothills, and survived by keeping herds of animals such as sheep and goats. People gradually moved south of the Himalayas, to areas where mighty rivers run through huge, fertile plains. Here, the climate enabled them to grow various crops.

India's climate is dominated by the monsoon, a wind that brings alternating seasons of hot, dry weather and heavy rain and flooding. In the drier west and north, wheat was the main crop from very early times, while higher rainfall in the east and south was ideal for growing rice. Rice cultivation was so successful in the plains around the Ganges river that many people settled there. This led to the growth of cities from around 300BC. Later, cities developed along rivers farther south.

From the 1st century AD, people no longer needed to make the overland journey into India. They came by ship from as far away as the Mediterranean Sea to ports on the west coast, in search of trade.

TRADING NATION
From 200BC, ancient India traded with the outside world by sea. They also bought and sold goods by land along the Silk Road – a route that cut across the Himalayas and through Central Asia to Samarkand and beyond.

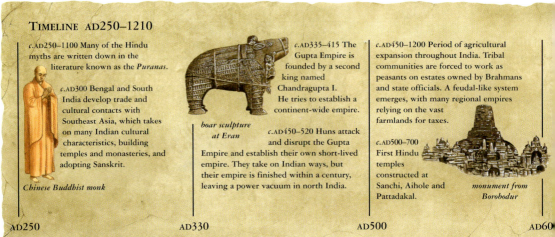

TIMELINE AD250–1210

c.AD250–1100 Many of the Hindu myths are written down in the literature known as the *Puranas*.

c.AD300 Bengal and South India develop trade and cultural contacts with Southeast Asia, which takes on many Indian cultural characteristics, building temples and monasteries, and adopting Sanskrit.

Chinese Buddhist monk

boar sculpture at Eran

c.AD335–415 The Gupta Empire is founded by a second king named Chandragupta I. He tries to establish a continent-wide empire.

c.AD450–520 Huns attack and disrupt the Gupta Empire and establish their own short-lived empire. They take on Indian ways, but their empire is finished within a century, leaving a power vacuum in north India.

c.AD450–1200 Period of agricultural expansion throughout India. Tribal communities are forced to work as peasants on estates owned by Brahmans and state officials. A feudal-like system emerges, with many regional empires relying on the vast farmlands for taxes.

c.AD500–700 First Hindu temples constructed at Sanchi, Aihole and Pattadakal.

monument from Borobodur

AD250　　　　　　AD330　　　　　　　AD500　　　　　　AD60

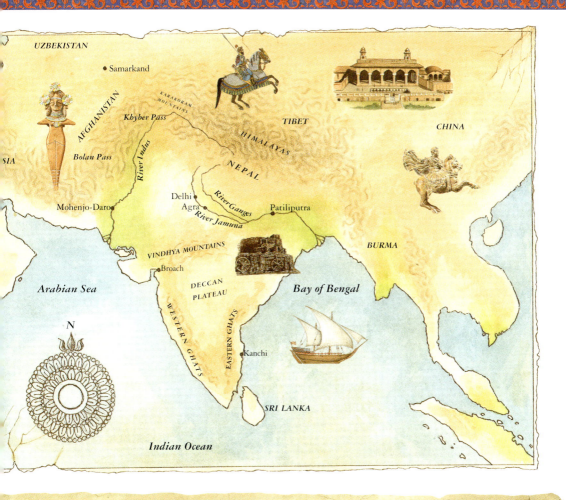

UZBEKISTAN

• Samarkand

AFGHANISTAN

KARAKORAM MOUNTAINS

Khyber Pass

TIBET

CHINA

Bolan Pass

SIA

HIMALAYAS

River Indus

NEPAL

Mohenjo-Daro•

Delhi •
Agra •
River Ganges
River Jamuna

Patiliputra

BURMA

VINDHYA MOUNTAINS

• Broach

DECCAN PLATEAU

Arabian Sea

WESTERN GHATS

EASTERN GHATS

Bay of Bengal

N

Kanchi

SRI LANKA

Indian Ocean

AD606–647 Harshavardhana, king of Kanauj, visited by Hsiuen-tsang. Splendors of courtly life and medieval culture flourish.

c.AD630–643 Chinese monk Hsiuen-tsang visits India to find Buddhism in decline in some areas.

Krishna dancing on serpent

c.AD712 Arab conquest of Sind by Muhammad Ibn Qasim after the local king refused to punish pirates who had abducted a shipful of orphans sent by the king of Sri Lanka to Baghdad.

c.AD752 King Dantidurga establishes a powerful empire in the Deccan, which is recognized by Arab geographers and travelers as one of the most powerful kingdoms in Asia.

Kailasanath temple at Ilora

AD997–1030 Sultan Mahmud of Ghazni makes 17 raids into northern India to loot temples of their wealth.

copper-plate inscription

c.AD1077 Embassy of merchants from the Chola dynasty of South India arrive at the Sung court in China.

AD1206 Aibak establishes the Sultanate in Delhi, the first Muslim kingdom in India.

AD700

AD900

AD1210

India's History Makers

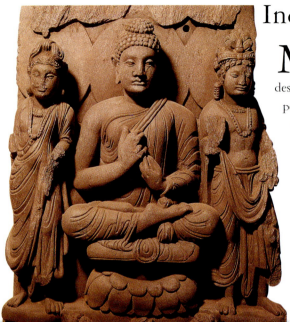

MANY OF THE REMARKABLE FIGURES of Indian history who shaped the country's destiny were great leaders. Ashoka was a powerful ruler 2,500 years ago who encouraged the spread of Buddhism. Many centuries later, Babur, a warlord from Samarkand in Central Asia, founded the Mughal Empire in India in the early 1500s. His grandson, Akbar, was a gifted politician and soldier who ruled for 49 years. The Mughal period was a time of huge development in the arts. Some Mughal rulers built magnificent cities, and many of their fine monuments and royal tombs can still be seen today.

From the time of the ancient civilization of the Aryans in the Indus Valley, religious teachers and scholars were respected. This may be because poverty and suffering have always been problems in India, which led people to think about why life was so difficult, and to seek ways of coping. Two of the most famous religious leaders are Gautama Buddha, who established the Buddhist way of life, and Guru Nanak, who founded the Sikh religion.

AN INFLUENTIAL LEADER
A statue of Gautama Buddha seated on a lotus flower. He founded Buddhism, which shaped life in India for thousands of years. Buddhism eventually died out in India, but it spread through many other parts of Asia. This created a link between India and many different eastern peoples and cultures.

TIMELINE AD1290–1870

1293 Marco Polo visits southern India. A flourishing trade is conducted throughout the Indian Ocean in silks, fabrics, spices and other luxuries.

1334–1370 The sultanate of Madurai, the southernmost Muslim kingdom, established briefly in southern India before being defeated by southern kingdoms.

stone chariot from Vijayanagar

c.1346–1565 The last great Hindu empire of Vijayanagar founded in southern India.

c.1360 Vedic and Hindu revival by the brothers Sayana and Madhava at the Vijayanagar court.

1398 The Mongol Timur devastates Delhi.

c.1440 Death of the Bhakti saint Kabir at Gorakhpur, where both Hindus and Muslims claim him as a great teacher.

tomb from the Sultanate period

1469–1539 Life of Guru Nanak, founder of Sikhism.

1498 Portuguese explorer Vasco da Gama visits Calicut.

1510 The Portugue conquer Goa.

1526 Babur, the Mongol, defeats the Sultan of Delhi and founds the Mogul empire.

Qutb Minar marble fountain

AD1290   AD1340   AD1400   AD152

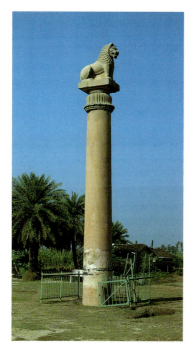

ROYAL HANDWRITING

This signature of Emperor Harsha (AD606–647) is carved in copper. Harsha was a patron (supporter) of arts and literature, and during his reign, the richness and elegance of the court reached new heights.

A SAINTLY LIFE

A statuette of Karaikal Ammaiyar, a woman who lived in southern India around AD600. She was so devoted to the god Shiva that she left her home and family, and gave her life entirely to him. She fasted as a symbol of her faith and became incredibly thin. Karaikal Ammaiyar is revered as a saint even today in southern India.

ART LOVER

Shah Jahan was one of the greatest statesmen of the Mughal Empire. He extended Mughal power south into the Deccan plateau and north into Afghanistan. However, he did not fulfil the Mughal dream of capturing the trading city of Samarkand, the "blue pearl of the Orient," in Central Asia. Shah Jahan was a great patron of architecture.

ASHOKA'S PILLAR

An edict (order) of Ashoka, ruler of India's first empire, is inscribed on this pillar. He published his edicts on pillars and rock faces throughout the land. Ashoka was a Buddhist. He claimed to have improved the lives of humans and animals, and had helped to spread justice.

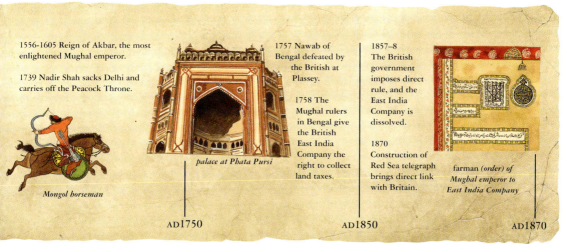

1556-1605 Reign of Akbar, the most enlightened Mughal emperor.

1739 Nadir Shah sacks Delhi and carries off the Peacock Throne.

Mongol horseman

palace at Phata Pursi

1757 Nawab of Bengal defeated by the British at Plassey.

1758 The Mughal rulers in Bengal give the British East India Company the right to collect land taxes.

1857–8 The British government imposes direct rule, and the East India Company is dissolved.

1870 Construction of Red Sea telegraph brings direct link with Britain.

farman (order) of Mughal emperor to East India Company

AD1750   AD1850   AD1870

The Chinese Empire

IMAGINE YOU COULD travel back in time 5,000 years and visit the lands of the Far East. In northern China you would come across smoky settlements of small thatched huts. You might see villagers fishing in rivers, sowing millet or baking pottery. From these small beginnings, China developed into an amazing civilization. Its towns grew into huge cities, with palaces and temples. Many Chinese became great writers, thinkers, artists, builders and inventors. China was first united under the rule of a single emperor in 221BC, and continued to be ruled by emperors until 1912.

China today is a modern country. Its ancient past has to be pieced together by archaeologists and historians. They dig up ancient tombs and settlements, and study textiles, ancient books and pottery. Their job is made easier because historical records were kept. These provide much information about the long history of Chinese civilization.

REST IN PEACE
A demon is trodden into defeat by a guardian spirit. Statues like this were commonly put in tombs to protect the dead against evil spirits.

ALL THE EMPEROR'S MEN
A vast model army marches again. It was dug up by archaeologists in 1974, and is now on display near Xian. The lifesize figures are made of terra-cotta (baked clay). They were buried in 210BC near the tomb of Qin Shi Huangdi, the first emperor of all China. He believed that they would protect him from evil spirits after he died.

TIMELINE 7000BC–110BC

Prehistoric remains of human ancestors dating back to 600,000BC have been found in China's Shaanxi province. The beginnings of Chinese civilization may be seen in the farming villages of the late Stone Age (8000BC–2500BC). As organized states grew up, the Chinese became skilled at warfare, working metals and making elaborate pottery and fine silk.

Banpo hut

c.7000BC Bands of hunters and fishers roam freely around the river valleys of China. They use simple stone tools and weapons.

c.3200BC Farming villages such as Banpo produce pottery in kilns. This way of life is called the Yangshao culture.

c.2100BC The start of a legendary 500-year period of rule, known as the Xia dynasty.

c.2000BC Black pottery is made by the people of the so-called Longshan culture.

Shang bronze vessel

c.1600BC Beginning of the Shang dynasty. Bronze worked and silk produced. The first picture-writing is used (on bones for telling fortunes).

1122BC Chou ruler Wu defeats Shang emperor. Wu becomes emperor of the Western Chou dynasty.

Zhou spearheads

| 7000BC | 2100BC | 1600BC | 780 |

A HEAVENLY HALL

The Hall of Prayer for Good Harvests (*shown right*) is part of Tiantan, the Temple of Heavenly Peace in Beijing. It was originally built in 1420, but had to be rebuilt in the 1890s after it was destroyed by lightning. Buildings like these tell us about traditional technology and design, as well as about Chinese religious beliefs.

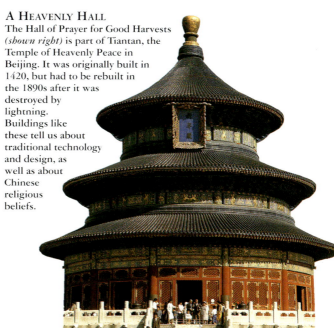

THE HAN EMPIRE (206BC–AD220)

China grew rapidly during the Han dynasty. By AD2 it had expanded to take in North Korea, the southeast coast, the southwest as far as Vietnam and large areas of Central Asia. Northern borders were defended by the Great Wall, which was extended during Han rule.

THE JADE PRINCE

In 1968, Chinese archaeologists excavated the tomb of Prince Liu Sheng. His remains were encased in a jade suit when he died in about 100BC. Over 2,400 pieces of this precious stone were joined with gold wire. It was believed that jade would preserve the body.

Chou soldier

771BC Capital city moves from Anyang to Luoyang. Beginning of Eastern Chou dynasty.

c.604BC Birth of the legendary Laozi, founder of Daoism.

551BC Teacher and philosopher Kong Fuzi (Confucius) born.

513BC Ironworking develops.

453BC Breakup of central rule. Small states fight each other for 200 years. Work begins on Grand Canal and Great Wall.

221BC China unites as a centralized empire under Zheng (Chiñ Shi Huangdi). Great Wall is extended.

213BC Chin Shi Huangdi burns all books that are not "practical."

Chinese writing

210BC Death of Chin Shi Huangdi. Terra cotta army guards his tomb, near Chang'an (modern Xian).

206BC Chin dynasty overthrown. Beginnings of Han dynasty as Xiang Yu and Liu Bang fight for control of the Han kingdom.

202BC The Western Han dynasty formally begins. It is led by the former official Liu Bang, who becomes emperor Gaozu.

200BC Chang'an becomes the capital of the Chinese Empire.

terra cotta warrior and horse

112BC Trade with the peoples of Western Asia and Europe begins to flourish along the Silk Road.

550BC   210BC   140BC   110BC

The Center of Civilization

CHINA IS A VAST COUNTRY, about the size of Europe. Its fertile plains and river valleys are ringed by many deserts and mountains. The ancient Chinese named their land Zhongguo, the Middle Kingdom, and believed that it was at the center of the civilized world. Most Chinese belong to a people called the Han, but the country is also inhabited by 50 or more different peoples, some of whom have played an important part in Chinese history. These groups include the Hui, Zhuang, Dai, Yao, Miao, Tibetans, Manchus and Mongols.

The very first Chinese civilizations grew up around the Huang He (Yellow River), where the fertile soil supported farming villages and then towns and cities. These became the centers of rival kingdoms. Between 1700BC and 256BC Chinese rule spread southward to the Chang Jiang (Yangzi River), the great river of Central China. All of eastern China was united within a single empire for the first time during Qin rule (221–206BC).

The rulers of the Han dynasty (206BC–AD220) then expanded the Empire southward as far as Vietnam. The Chinese Empire was now even larger than the Roman Empire, dominating Central and Southeast Asia. The Mongols, from lands to the north of China, ruled the Empire from 1279 to 1368. They were succeeded by the Ming dynasty, which was in turn overthown by the Manchu in 1644. In later centuries, China became inward-looking and unable to resist interference from Europe. The Empire finally collapsed, with China declaring itself a republic in 1912.

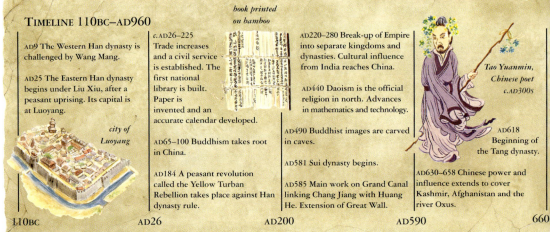

TIMELINE 110BC–AD960

AD9 The Western Han dynasty is challenged by Wang Mang.

AD25 The Eastern Han dynasty begins under Liu Xiu, after a peasant uprising. Its capital is at Luoyang.

city of Luoyang

c.AD26–225 Trade increases and a civil service is established. The first national library is built. Paper is invented and an accurate calendar developed.

book printed on bamboo

AD65–100 Buddhism takes root in China.

AD184 A peasant revolution called the Yellow Turban Rebellion takes place against Han dynasty rule.

AD220–280 Break-up of Empire into separate kingdoms and dynasties. Cultural influence from India reaches China.

AD440 Daoism is the official religion in north. Advances in mathematics and technology.

AD490 Buddhist images are carved in caves.

AD581 Sui dynasty begins.

AD585 Main work on Grand Canal linking Chang Jiang with Huang He. Extension of Great Wall.

Tao Yuanmin, Chinese poet c.AD300s

AD618 Beginning of the Tang dynasty.

AD630–658 Chinese power and influence extends to cover Kashmir, Afghanistan and the river Oxus.

110BC   AD26   AD200   AD590   660

Mongol warrior

CENTRAL ASIA

Caspian Sea

MONGOLIA

Gobi Desert

The Great Wall

Beijing

Chang'an (Xian)

Grand Canal

Huang He

JAPAN

Hangzhou

Chang Jiang

Chinese junk

trader on Silk Road

Persian Gulf

Himalaya Mountains

rice

River Ganges

ARABIA

Arabian Sea

INDIA

Bay of Bengal

SOUTHEAST ASIA

South China Sea

flying fish

TRADING EMPIRE
The map shows the extent of the Chinese Empire during the Ming dynasty (1368–1644). Merchants transported luxury Chinese goods along the Silk Road, which stretched from Chang'an (Xian) to Mediterranean countries. Sea routes took traders to Vietnam, Korea and Japan.

the Great Buddha of Leshan

AD751 Battle of Talas River settles China's borders with Islamic lands to west.

AD755 Rebellion and civil war in northern China.

AD762 Death of the poet Li Bai.

AD770 Death of the poet Du Fu.

AD840s Spread of Islam in China.

c.AD850 Chinese use gunpowder to make the first fireworks.

AD868 The first book is printed by woodblock.

AD906 China breaks up into different kingdoms.

AD939 Annam (Vietnam) becomes independent from China.

AD660–705 Rule of Wu Zetian.

AD712 Start of a golden age of Chinese arts and literature. China becomes the most powerful nation in the world under the Tang emperor Xuanzong.

AD713–803 Great Buddha carved from the cliff at Leshan.

Great Hall of the Nandan temple, Shaanxi

Chinese fireworks

AD947 Khitan people overrun northern China.

AD750   AD840   AD940   AD960

People of the Chinese Empire

GREAT EMPIRES ARE made by ordinary people as much as by their rulers. The Chinese empire could not have been built without the millions of peasants who planted crops, built defensive walls and dug canals. The names of these people are largely forgotten, except for those who led uprisings and revolts against their rulers. The inventors, thinkers, artists, poets and writers of imperial China are better known. They had a great effect on the society they lived in, and left behind ideas, works of art and inventions that still influence people today.

The royal court was made up of thousands of officials, artists, craftsmen and servants. Some had great political power. China's rulers came from many different backgrounds and peoples.

LAOZI (born *c.*604BC)
The legendary Laozi is said to have been a scholar who worked as a court librarian. It is thought that he wrote the book known as the *Daodejing*. He believed people should live in harmony with nature, and his ideas later formed the basis of Daoism.

Many emperors were ruthless former warlords who were hungry for power. Others are remembered as scholars or artists. Some women also achieved great political influence, openly or from behind the scenes.

KONG FUZI (551–479BC)
Kong Fuzi is better known in the West by the Latin version of his name, Confucius. He was a public official who became an influential teacher and thinker. His views on family life, society and the treatment of others greatly influenced later generations.

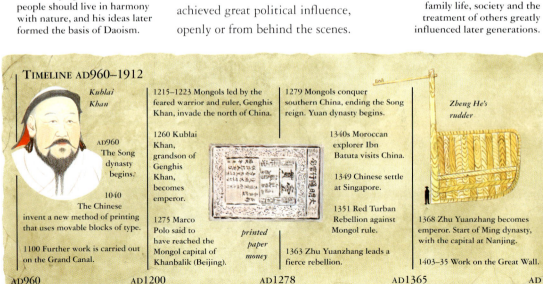

TIMELINE AD960–1912

Kublai Khan

AD960 The Song dynasty begins.

1040 The Chinese invent a new method of printing that uses movable blocks of type.

1100 Further work is carried out on the Grand Canal.

1215–1223 Mongols led by the feared warrior and ruler, Genghis Khan, invade the north of China.

1260 Kublai Khan, grandson of Genghis Khan, becomes emperor.

1275 Marco Polo said to have reached the Mongol capital of Khanbalik (Beijing).

printed paper money

1279 Mongols conquer southern China, ending the Song reign. Yuan dynasty begins.

1340s Moroccan explorer Ibn Batuta visits China.

1349 Chinese settle at Singapore.

1351 Red Turban Rebellion against Mongol rule.

1363 Zhu Yuanzhang leads a fierce rebellion.

Zheng He's rudder

1368 Zhu Yuanzhang becomes emperor. Start of Ming dynasty, with the capital at Nanjing.

1403–35 Work on the Great Wall.

AD960   AD1200   AD1278   AD1365   AD1

HAN GAOZU (256–195BC)

In the Chin dynasty (221–206BC) Liu Bang was a minor public official in charge of a relay station for royal messengers. He watched as the centralized Chin Empire fell apart. In 206BC he declared himself ruler of the Han kingdom. In 202BC he defeated his opponent, Xiang Yu, and founded the Han dynasty. As emperor Gaozu, he tried to unite China without using Chin's harsh methods.

CHIN SHI HUANGDI (256–210BC)

Scholars plead for their lives before the first emperor. Zheng came to the throne of a state called Chin at the age of nine. He went on to rule all China and was given his full title, meaning First Emperor of Chin. His brutal methods included burying his opponents alive.

EMPRESS WU ZETIAN
(AD624–705)

The emperor Tang Gaozong enraged officials when he replaced his legal wife with Wu, his concubine (secondary wife). After the emperor suffered a stroke in AD660, Wu took control of the country. In AD690 she became the only woman in history to declare herself empress of China.

KUBLAI KHAN (AD1214–1294)

The explorer Marco Polo was said to have visited emperor Kublai Khan at Khanbalik (Beijing). Kublai Khan was a Mongol who conquered northern, and later southern, China.

1405–33 Chinese voyages of exploration under Zheng He.

1421 Beijing becomes the capital city of the Chinese Empire.

Manchu warrior

1428 The Chinese are expelled from Annam (Vietnam).

1550 Japanese pirates mount raids on China. Mongols invade north again.

1644 Li Zicheng leads a rebellion against Ming rule. Manchu invasion. Ching dynasty founded.

Boxer rebels

1673 Rebellions against Ching rule in south.

1839–42 First Opium War. Britain forces China to accept opium imports from India.

1842 Treaty of Nanjing. Britain gains Hong Kong.

1850–64 Taiping rebellion.

1858 Treaty of Tianjin. Chinese ports taken over by foreign powers.

1862 The Empress Dowager Cixi becomes regent.

1894–5 War with Japan. Loss of Taiwan.

1899–1900 Boxer Rebellion against Ching and foreign governments.

1908 Last emperor, Puyi, ascends to throne as a small boy.

Puyi, the last emperor

1912 Declaration of republic by Sun Yatsen. Emperor Puyi abdicates.

AD1425   AD1650   AD1880   AD1912

A Golden Age in Greece

O N THE SHORES of the eastern Mediterranean, 3,000 years ago, one of the most enduring and influential civilizations of the Western world emerged. Ancient Greece was made up of a number of self-supporting city-states, each of which developed a strong, individual identity. They developed from an agricultural society that wrote in simple pictograms into a sophisticated culture. Centuries on, the Greek legacy survives in parts of modern society. The origins of democracy, mathematics, medicine and philosophy can be traced back to this time in history. Even some of our modern words are made up from ancient Greek. "Telephone" comes from the ancient Greek words "tele" meaning far and "phonos" meaning sound.

A FEAT OF PERFECTION
The Parthenon is regarded as the supreme achievement of Greek architecture. It was the most important building in Athens, where it still sits on top of the Acropolis. The temple took 15 years to build and was dedicated to Athena, guardian goddess of Athens. Around 24,000 tons of marble, transported from over 9 miles away, were used in its construction.

TIMELINE 40,000BC–1100BC

The first people lived in Greece about 40,000 years ago. They lived in a tribal, hunter-gatherer society. Settlements and the beginning of farming did not occur until 6,000BC. The first great Greek civilization, and also the first in Europe, flourished on the island of Crete around 2000BC. This was the mighty Minoan civilization whose decline heralded in the glorious age of the Mycenaeans. After this a period known as the Dark Ages began. It was followed by the golden age of Classical Greece which lasted from about 500BC to 336BC.

a drinking vessel (rhyton) in the shape of a bull's head from Knossos

c.6000BC The first settlers arrive on the island of Crete and the Greek mainland.

c.2900–1000BC The Bronze Age in Greece. People discover how to mix copper and tin to make bronze.

disk from Crete with unique pictographic script

c.2000BC Minoan civilization flourishes on Crete. The Minoans use a script called Linear A, which has not yet been deciphered.

c.1600BC The Mycenaeans dominate mainland Greece.

statuette of worshipping woman from Mycenae

40,000BC   6000BC   2000BC   1

THE ANCIENT GREEK WORLD

The map above shows the main ports and cities through which the Greeks traded. The ancient Greek world centered on the Aegean Sea, but the Greeks were adventurous seafarers. Trade took them from the Aegean Sea to the Atlantic Ocean and the shores of the Black Sea, where they formed many settlements. These colonies helped Greece to spread its influence beyond the mainland and its offshore islands.

CENTER STONE

The omphalos was a carved stone kept at the shrine at Delphi. The ancient Greeks thought that this holy sanctuary was the center of the world. The omphalos stone was placed there to mark the center. It was said to have been put there by Zeus, ruler of the gods. It may have also served as an altar on which sacrifices were made.

THE PAST REVEALED

Archaeological evidence in the shape of pottery such as this vase help us to piece together the history of Greece. This vase is typical of the superior craftsmanship for which the Greeks were admired. It was common for vases to be decorated with pictures showing historical events. In this one, we see a scene from the siege of Troy in which the king is being murdered. The siege was an important event in Greek folklore. These decorative vases were used as containers for liquids such as oil, water and wine. The export of such pottery contributed an enormous amount of wealth to the Greeks.

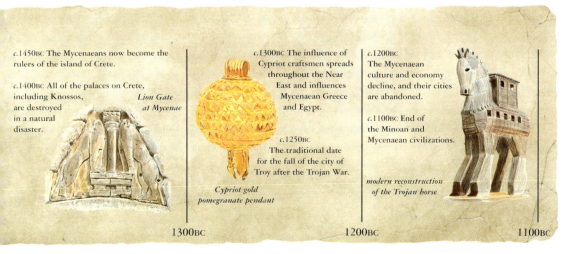

*c.*1450BC The Mycenaeans now become the rulers of the island of Crete.

*c.*1400BC All of the palaces on Crete, including Knossos, are destroyed in a natural disaster.

Lion Gate at Mycenae

*c.*1300BC The influence of Cypriot craftsmen spreads throughout the Near East and influences Mycenaean Greece and Egypt.

*c.*1250BC
The traditional date for the fall of the city of Troy after the Trojan War.

Cypriot gold pomegranate pendant

*c.*1200BC
The Mycenaean culture and economy decline, and their cities are abandoned.

*c.*1100BC End of the Minoan and Mycenaean civilizations.

modern reconstruction of the Trojan horse

1300BC   1200BC   1100BC

Greek Civilizations

T HE HISTORY OF ANCIENT GREECE spans 20 centuries. It starts with the Minoan civilization on the island of Crete, which reached its height between 1900 and 1450BC. This culture was also the first to develop in Europe. The Minoans were a lively and artistic people who built palaces and towns and were also great seafarers. Their achievements greatly influenced the Mycenaeans, who built their own civilization on the Greek mainland from around 1600BC. Both the Minoan and Mycenaean cultures collapsed, probably under the impact of natural disasters and warfare, and were followed by centuries of poverty.

Revival was under way by 750BC, and the Greek world reached its economic peak during the 5th century BC. This period is known as the Classical Age, when Athens was at the height of its power and prosperity. During this century, Athens led the Greeks into many victorious battles against Persia. However, Athens itself later suffered an economic decline because of a series of wars fought against its rival, Sparta. Then, in the 4th century BC, Greece was conquered by Macedonia. The Macedonian ruler, Alexander the Great, spread Greek culture throughout his empire. Finally, between 168 and 146BC Macedonia and Greece were absorbed into the Roman Empire, and Greek civilization became part of the heritage that Rome passed on to the rest of Europe.

TRADE AND EXPANSION
The Classical Age in Greek history dates from around 500 to 336BC. This period was marked by an increase in the wealth of most Greek city-states. Greek trade ships were sailing throughout the Mediterranean and Black Sea. Colonies were also being set up on the shorelines of these two seas.

ITALY

• *Locri*

SICILY

• *Naxos*

• *Syracuse*

N

W

S

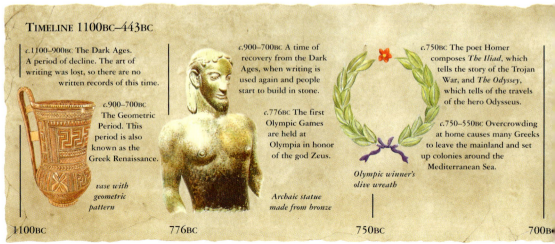

TIMELINE 1100BC–443BC

*c.*1100–900BC The Dark Ages. A period of decline. The art of writing was lost, so there are no written records of this time.

*c.*900–700BC The Geometric Period. This period is also known as the Greek Renaissance.

vase with geometric pattern

*c.*900–700BC A time of recovery from the Dark Ages, when writing is used again and people start to build in stone.

*c.*776BC The first Olympic Games are held at Olympia in honor of the god Zeus.

Archaic statue made from bronze

Olympic winner's olive wreath

*c.*750BC The poet Homer composes *The Iliad*, which tells the story of the Trojan War, and *The Odyssey*, which tells of the travels of the hero Odysseus.

*c.*750–550BC Overcrowding at home causes many Greeks to leave the mainland and set up colonies around the Mediterranean Sea.

1100BC   776BC   750BC   700BC

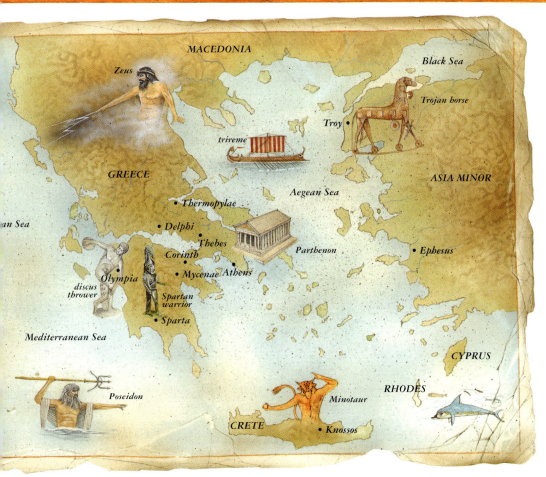

MACEDONIA

Zeus

Black Sea

Trojan horse

trireme

Troy •

GREECE

ASIA MINOR

Aegean Sea

• *Thermopylae*

• *Delphi*

• *Thebes*

Corinth

Parthenon

• *Ephesus*

discus thrower

Olympia

• *Mycenae*   *Athens*

Spartan warrior

• *Sparta*

an Sea

Mediterranean Sea

CYPRUS

Poseidon

RHODES

Minotaur

CRETE   • *Knossos*

*c.*700–500BC **The Archaic Period.** During this period Greece expands. Athens becomes the largest and most influential of the independent city-states that make up Greece.

*c.*508BC **Democracy is introduced in Athens.** Every citizen has the right to speak and vote.

Odysseus gouges out the eye of a Cyclops

*c.*500–336BC **The Classical Age.** Greek culture and learning reaches its height.

*c.*480–479BC **The Persian Wars.** The Greeks are victorious, defeating the Persians at the battles of Marathon and Salamis.

Persian archer

*c.*479–431BC **The golden age of Athens.** Trade flourishes and the city grows very prosperous.

*c.*447–432BC **The Parthenon is built in Athens.**

the Parthenon

500BC   479BC   443BC

Heroes of Greek Society

THE GREEKS TREASURED THEIR rich store of myths and legends about the gods, but they also took a keen interest in human history. They valued fame and glory far more than riches. Their ultimate aim in life was to make a name for themselves that would live on long after death. Statues were put up in prominent places to honor Greeks who had won fame in different ways – as generals on the battlefield, as poets, teachers, philosophers, mathematicians, orators or sportsmen. These heroes represented the human qualities the Greeks most admired – physical courage, endurance and strength, and the intelligence to create, invent, explain and persuade.

HOMER (c700BC)
The blind poet Homer (above) was honored for writing two epic tales. The first is *The Iliad,* a story about the siege of Troy. The other is *The Odyssey* which follows the adventures of Odysseus in his travels after the battle of Troy. Scholars now believe that the tales may have been written by two poets or even groups of several poets.

SAPPHO (c600BC)
The poet Sappho was born on the island of Lesbos. She wrote nine books of poetry, but only one complete poem survives. Beauty and love were the subjects of her poetry. Her work inspired other artists of the time and influenced many writers and poets in later centuries.

SOPHOCLES (496–406BC)
Only seven of Sophocles' plays have survived. He is thought to have written 123 altogether. Besides being a playwright, Sophocles was also a respected general and politician. His name means "famed for wisdom".

TIMELINE 443BC–140BC

443–429BC The great statesman, Pericles, dominates politics in Athens.

431–404BC The Peloponnesian Wars take place between Athens and its great rival, Sparta. The Spartans defeat the Athenians.

399BC The Athenian philosopher, Socrates is condemned to death because his views prove unpopular.

marble bust of the philosopher, Socrates

371BC Sparta is defeated by Thebes. Thebes becomes the leading power in Greece.

362BC Sparta and Athens combine forces to defeat the Thebans at the battle of Mantinea.

338BC The Greeks are defeated by the Macedonians at the battle of Chaeronea. Philip II of Macedonia becomes ruler of Greece.

iron corselet, which is thought to have belonged to Philip II of Macedonia

336BC Philip II of Macedonia dies and is succeeded by his son, Alexander the Great. Alexander builds a huge empire, stretching from Greece as far east as India.

bronze statuette of Alexander the Great

443BC   371BC   336BC   334BC

PERICLES (495–429BC)

A popular figure and brilliant public speaker, Pericles was elected as a general 20 times. While in office, he built up a powerful navy and organized the building of strong defenses, beautiful temples and fine monuments. He also gave ordinary citizens more say in government. Pericles' career ended after he led Athens into a disastrous war against Sparta. He was ostracized (expelled) as punishment for his misjudgment.

ALEXANDER THE GREAT (356–323BC)

Alexander was the son of Philip II of Macedonia. His life was spent in conquest of new territory, and his empire stretched across the Middle East, Persia and Afghanistan as far as the river Indus. His empire was swiftly divided when he died after suspected poisoning.

SOCRATES (469–399BC)

A renowned teacher and philosopher, Socrates encouraged people to think about how to live a good life. The Athenians sentenced him to die by drinking hemlock (a poison). Plato, Socrates' most brilliant pupil and himself a great philosopher, recorded his teacher's last days.

ARCHIMEDES (287–211BC)

The mathematician, scientist, astronomer and inventor, Archimedes came from Syracuse. When his city was besieged by the Romans, he designed a huge lens that focused sunlight on the Roman ships and set them on fire. He also devised a screw for raising water out of the ground and studied the concepts of floating and balance.

334BC Alexander the Great invades Persia to include it in his empire.

333BC The Persian army, led by King Darius, is defeated by Alexander the Great at the battle of Issus.

331BC Alexander the Great becomes king of Persia after defeating the Persians at the battle of Gaugamela.

King Darius of Persia

Romulus and Remus, legendary founders of Rome

323BC Alexander the Great dies, and his successors fight over the throne.

275BC Greek colonies are taken over by the Romans.

168BC Rome defeats the Macedonian rulers of Greece.

147–146BC The Achaean War. The Romans take control of Greece and Macedonia.

Roman soldier in full armor

323BC   168BC   146BC

Rome: From City to Empire

T HE CITY OF ROME today is a bustling place, full of traffic and crowds. But if you could travel back in time to around 800BC, you would find only a few small villages on peaceful, wooded hillsides along the banks of the river Tiber. According to legend, Rome was founded here in 753BC. In the centuries that followed, the Romans came to dominate Italy and the Mediterranean. They farmed and traded and fought for new lands. Rome grew to become the center of a vast empire that stretched across Europe into Africa and Asia. The Empire lasted for centuries and brought a sophisticated way of life to vast numbers of people. Many Roman buildings and artifacts still survive to show us what life was like in the Roman Empire.

ROMAN ITALY
As the city of Rome prospered, the Romans gradually conquered neighboring tribes. By 250BC they controlled most of Italy. This map shows some of the important towns and cities of that time.

ANCIENT AND MODERN
In Rome today, people live alongside the temples, marketplaces and public buildings of the past. This is the Colosseum, a huge arena called an amphitheater. It was used for staging games and fights, and first opened to the public in AD80.

TIMELINE 750BC–300BC

Rome's rise to power was sudden and spectacular. Its eventful history includes bloody battles, eccentric emperors, amazing inventions and remarkable feats of engineering. The Roman Empire prospered for almost 500 years, and still influences the way we live today.

Romulus, the first king of Rome

c.753BC The city of Rome is founded by Romulus, according to legend.

673–641BC Tullus Hostilius, Rome's third king, expands the city's territory by conquering a neighboring settlement. Rome's population doubles as a result.

641–616BC Pons Sublicius, the first bridge across the river Tiber, is constructed. The harbor town of Ostia is founded at the mouth of the Tiber.

600BC The Latin language is first written in a script that is still used today.

inscription in Latin, carved in stone

750BC   753BC   600BC   55

CLUES TO THE PAST

The coin on this necklace dates from the reign of the Emperor Domitian, AD81–96. Gold does not rot like wood and other materials, so jewelry like this can give us clues about Roman craft methods, changing fashions, trade and even warfare.

SECRETS BENEATH THE SEA

Divers have discovered Roman shipwrecks deep under the waters of the Mediterranean Sea. Many have their cargo still intact. These jars were being transported over 2,000 years ago. By examining shipwrecks, archaeologists can learn how Roman boats were built, what they carried and where they traded.

ARCHAEOLOGISTS AT WORK

These archaeologists are excavating sections of wall plaster from the site of a Roman house in Britain. Many remains of Roman buildings and artifacts, as well as books and other documents, have survived from that time. These all help us build up a picture of what life was like in the Roman Empire.

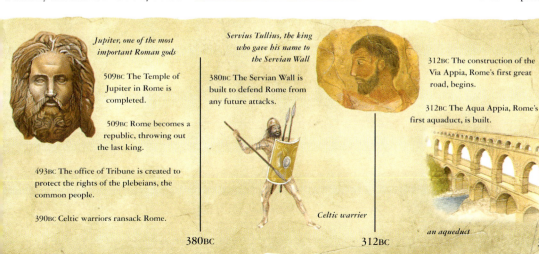

Jupiter, one of the most important Roman gods

509BC The Temple of Jupiter in Rome is completed.

509BC Rome becomes a republic, throwing out the last king.

493BC The office of Tribune is created to protect the rights of the plebeians, the common people.

390BC Celtic warriors ransack Rome.

Servius Tullius, the king who gave his name to the Servian Wall

380BC The Servian Wall is built to defend Rome from any future attacks.

312BC The construction of the Via Appia, Rome's first great road, begins.

312BC The Aqua Appia, Rome's first aquaduct, is built.

Celtic warrior

an aqueduct

380BC   312BC   300BC

The Vast Roman Empire

BRITAIN
London
FRANCE
SPAIN

BY THE YEAR AD117, the Roman Empire was at its height. It was possible to travel nearly 2,500 miles from east to west and still hear the trumpets of the Roman legions. As a Roman soldier you might have had to shiver in the snowy winters of northern Britain, or sweat and toil in the heat of the Egyptian desert.

The peoples of the Empire were very different. There were Greeks, Egyptians, Syrians, Jews, Africans, Germans and Celts. Many of them belonged to civilizations that were already ancient when Rome was still a group of villages. Many revolted against Roman rule, but uprisings were quickly put down. Gradually, conquered peoples came to accept being part of the Empire. From AD212 onward, any free person living under Roman rule had the right to claim "I am a Roman citizen." Slaves, however, had very few rights.

In AD284, after a series of violent civil wars, this vast empire was divided into several parts. Despite being reunited by the Emperor Constantine in AD324, the Empire was doomed. A hundred years later, the western part was invaded by fierce warriors from the north, with disastrous consequences. Although the Western Empire came to an end in AD476, the eastern part continued until 1453. The Latin language survived, used by the Roman Catholic Church and by scientists and scholars in Europe. It is still learned today, and is the basis of languages such as Italian, Spanish, French and Romanian.

TIMELINE 300BC–1BC

264BC First record of a gladiatorial contest.

264–241BC The first of three wars between Rome and Carthage, which came to be known as the Punic Wars.

250BC Rome controls most of Italy.

a gladiator

one of Hannibal's war elephants

240BC The first Roman dramas are performed on stage.

218–201BC Second war between Rome and Carthage. Hannibal, a Carthaginian general, crosses the Alps by elephant.

c.211BC The first Roman silver coin, *denarius*, is minted at Rome.

206BC Rome conquers Iberia (present-day Spain).

200BC The Romans are using concrete in buildings.

196BC Rome defeats the Macedonian rulers of Greece. Triumphal arches are built in Rome.

a triumphal arch, built to celebrate a victory

300BC

240BC

206BC

19

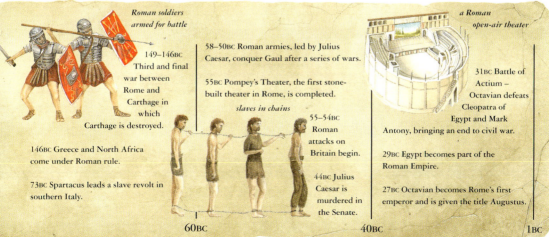

GERMANY

Caspian Sea

Black Sea

ITALY
River Tiber
CORSICA
Rome
SARDINIA
Mediterranean Sea
SICILY
Carthage
NORTH AFRICA

GREECE

TURKEY
SYRIA
CYPRUS
Mediterranean Sea
CRETE

EGYPT
River Nile
Red Sea

The extent of the Roman Empire in AD117

THE HUGE EMPIRE

The Roman Empire reached its greatest size in AD117. This map shows its extent, stretching thousands of miles to the east, west, north and south. Present-day names are used on the map to help compare the Empire to Europe and the Middle East today.

Roman soldiers armed for battle

149–146BC Third and final war between Rome and Carthage in which Carthage is destroyed.

146BC Greece and North Africa come under Roman rule.

73BC Spartacus leads a slave revolt in southern Italy.

58–50BC Roman armies, led by Julius Caesar, conquer Gaul after a series of wars.

55BC Pompey's Theater, the first stone-built theater in Rome, is completed.

slaves in chains

55–54BC Roman attacks on Britain begin.

44BC Julius Caesar is murdered in the Senate.

a Roman open-air theater

31BC Battle of Actium – Octavian defeats Cleopatra of Egypt and Mark Antony, bringing an end to civil war.

29BC Egypt becomes part of the Roman Empire.

27BC Octavian becomes Rome's first emperor and is given the title Augustus.

60BC — 40BC — 1BC

History Makers of Rome

T HE PEOPLE who made Roman history came from many different backgrounds. The names of the famous survive on monuments and in books. There were consuls and emperors, successful generals and powerful politicians, great writers and historians. However, it was thousands of ordinary people who really kept the Roman Empire going – merchants, soldiers of the legions, tax collectors, servants, farmers, potters, and others like them.

Many of the most famous names of that time were not Romans at all. There was the Carthaginian general, Hannibal, Rome's deadliest enemy. There were also Celtic chieftains and queens, such as Vercingetorix, Caractacus and Boudicca.

AUGUSTUS (63BC–AD14)
Augustus, born Octavian, was the great-nephew and adopted son of Julius Caesar. After Caesar's death, he took control of the army. He became ruler of the Roman world after defeating Mark Antony at the Battle of Actium in 31BC. In 27BC, he became Rome's first emperor and was given the title Augustus.

ROMULUS AND REMUS
According to legend, Romulus was the founder and first king of Rome. The legend tells how he and his twin brother Remus were abandoned as babies. They were saved by a she-wolf, who looked after them until they were found by a shepherd.

CICERO (106–43BC)
Cicero is remembered as Rome's greatest orator, or speaker. Many of his letters and speeches still survive. He was a writer, poet, politican, lawyer and philosopher. He was elected consul of Rome in 63BC, but he had many enemies and was murdered in 43BC.

TIMELINE AD1–AD476

AD43 The Roman conquest of Britain begins.

AD50 Rome is the largest city in the world – population about 1 million. Roman traders reach Bengal and India.

AD60 Queen Boudicca leads an uprising in Britain.

AD64 The Great Fire of Rome.

AD75 Rome sets up trade links across the Sahara.

Vesuvius begins to erupt

AD79 The volcano Vesuvius erupts, burying Pompeii and Herculaneum.

AD117 The Roman Empire is at its largest.

AD118–128 The Pantheon in Rome is built.

AD122 Work begins on Hadrian's Wall, a defensive barrier across northern Britain.

AD165–167 Plague spreads through the Empire.

c.AD200 Road system covers all parts of the Empire.

AD212 All free people in the Empire are granted citizenship.

the Pantheon in Rome

AD1   AD75   AD150   AD2

Boudicca, queen of the Iceni in Britain

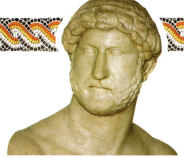

HADRIAN (AD76–138)

Hadrian became emperor in AD117 and spent many years traveling around the Empire. He had many splendid buildings constructed, as well as a defensive barrier across northern Britain, now known as Hadrian's Wall.

NERO (AD37–68) AND AGRIPPINA

In AD54 Nero became emperor after the death of his adoptive father Claudius. A cruel ruler, he was blamed for a great fire that destroyed much of Rome in AD64. Agrippina, his mother, was a powerful influence on him. She was suspected of poisoning two of her three husbands, and was eventually killed on her son's orders.

CLEOPATRA (68–30BC)

An Egyptian queen of Greek descent, Cleopatra had a son by Julius Caesar. She then fell in love with Mark Antony, a close follower of Caesar. They joined forces against Rome, but after a crushing defeat at Actium in 31BC, they both committed suicide. Egypt then became part of the Roman Empire.

JULIUS CAESAR (100–44BC)

Caesar was a talented and popular general and politician. He led Roman armies in an eight-year campaign to conquer Gaul (present-day France) in 50BC. In 49BC, he used his victorious troops to seize power and declare himself dictator for life. Five years later he was stabbed to death in the Senate by fellow politicians.

---

the cross, a symbol of Christianity

AD270 A new defensive wall is built around Rome by the Emperor Aurelian.

AD284 New laws and taxes. Divisions in the Empire appear.

AD313 Christianity is made legal.

AD324 The Emperor Constantine reunites the Empire and founds Constantinople (present-day Istanbul, in Turkey).

AD330 Constantinople becomes Constantine's new capital in the east.

AD395 The Roman Empire is divided into two parts – Eastern and Western.

the Emperor Constantine, depicted on a Roman coin

AD410 The city of Rome is raided and ransacked by Visigoth armies from Germany.

Vandal warrior

AD455 Vandal armies from Germany ransack Rome.

AD476 Fall of the Western Empire – the Eastern Empire survives until 1453.

AD330   AD400   AD476

The Coming of the Vikings

THE YEAR IS AD795. Imagine you are an Irish monk, gathering herbs to make medicines. Walking along the river bank you hear the sound of creaking oars and curses in a strange language. Through the reeds you see a long wooden ship slipping upstream. It has a prow carved like a dragon. Inside it are fierce-looking men – battle-scarred warriors, armed with swords and axes.

Incidents like this happened time after time around the coasts of Europe in the years that followed. In the West, these invaders were called Northmen, Norsemen or Danes. In the East, they were known as Rus or Varangians. They have gone down in history as Vikings. This name comes from a word in the Old Norse language meaning sea raiding. Who were they? The Vikings were Scandinavians from the lands known today as Denmark, Norway and Sweden. Archaeologists have found their farms and houses, the goods they traded, the treasure they stole and their fine wooden ships.

BATTLE ART
The Vikings were skilled artists, as well as fierce warriors. This Danish battle ax is made of iron inlaid with silver. It has been decorated with beautiful swirling patterns.

INTO THE PAST
Archaeologists have excavated Viking towns and found ships, weapons and hoards of treasure. This excavation is in York, in northern England.

SEAFARERS
The outline of the Viking ship, with its high prow and square sail, became widely feared. This carving is from the Swedish island of Gotland.

TIMELINE AD750–875

The Vikings were descended from German tribes who moved northward into Scandinavia. They were restless, energetic people. By the AD780s, they were raiding other lands. Soon they were exploring, settling and trading far from home, from North America to Baghdad. By 1100 the Vikings had become Christian and their lands had become more like the other countries in western Europe.

Viking sword

AD750 Trade opens up between northern Europe and the East. Trading routes are established.

c.AD750 Small trading and manufacturing towns flourish, such as Ribe in Denmark, Paviken on Gotland and Helgo in Sweden.

treasure hoard

AD789 Vikings raid southern England.

AD793 Vikings raid Lindisfarne, an island off the northeast coast of England.

massacre at Lindisfarne

AD795 Vikings raid Scotland and Ireland.

AD750   AD775   AD8

THE VIKING HOMELANDS

The Vikings came from Scandinavia. This map shows some of the most important Viking sites. Most of these were in present-day Denmark, southern Sweden and along Norway's coastal fjords.

INVASION FLEET

The Vikings invaded England in AD866. They went on to defeat and murder Edmund, King of the East Angles. Much of our knowledge of the Vikings comes from accounts written by their enemies. Many of these, such as this one about the life of St. Edmund, were written later.

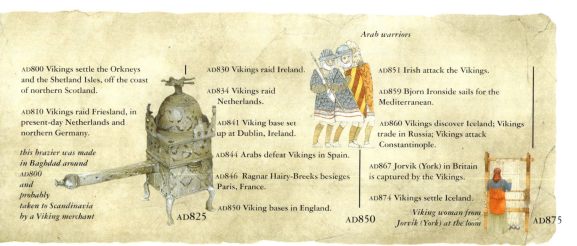

AD800 Vikings settle the Orkneys and the Shetland Isles, off the coast of northern Scotland.

AD810 Vikings raid Friesland, in present-day Netherlands and northern Germany.

this brazier was made in Baghdad around AD800 and probably taken to Scandinavia by a Viking merchant

AD825

Arab warriors

AD830 Vikings raid Ireland.

AD834 Vikings raid Netherlands.

AD841 Viking base set up at Dublin, Ireland.

AD844 Arabs defeat Vikings in Spain.

AD846 Ragnar Hairy-Breeks besieges Paris, France.

AD850 Viking bases in England.

AD850

AD851 Irish attack the Vikings.

AD859 Bjorn Ironside sails for the Mediterranean.

AD860 Vikings discover Iceland; Vikings trade in Russia; Vikings attack Constantinople.

AD867 Jorvik (York) in Britain is captured by the Vikings.

AD874 Vikings settle Iceland.

Viking woman from Jorvik (York) at the loom

AD875

The Viking World

THE VIKINGS took to the sea in search of wealth, fortune and better land for farming. At that time, Denmark was mostly rough heath or woodland. The other Viking homelands of Norway and Sweden were harsh landscapes, with mountains and dense forests, which were difficult to farm.

From the AD780s onward, bands of Vikings launched savage attacks on England, Scotland, Ireland and Wales. They later settled large areas of the British Isles, including the Orkneys, Shetlands and the Isle of Man. Viking raiders also attacked settlements along the coasts and rivers of Germany, the Netherlands and France. The area they settled in France became known as Normandy, meaning land of the Northmen.

Viking warriors sailed as far as Spain, where they clashed with the Arabs who then ruled it. They also traveled west across the Atlantic Ocean, settling in Iceland, Greenland and even North America.

Viking traders founded states in the Ukraine and Russia and sailed down the rivers of eastern Europe. They hired themselves out as the emperor's bodyguards in the city they called Miklagard – also known as Constantinople (modern Istanbul).

By the 1100s, the descendants of the Vikings lived in powerful Christian kingdoms. The wild days of piracy were over.

N

L'Anse aux Meadows

NEWFOUNDL
(VINLA

CANADA

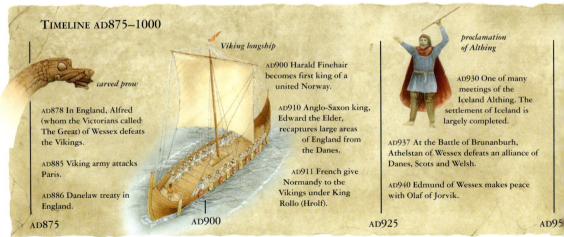

TIMELINE AD875–1000

Viking longship

carved prow

proclamation of Althing

AD878 In England, Alfred (whom the Victorians called The Great) of Wessex defeats the Vikings.

AD885 Viking army attacks Paris.

AD886 Danelaw treaty in England.

AD900 Harald Finehair becomes first king of a united Norway.

AD910 Anglo-Saxon king, Edward the Elder, recaptures large areas of England from the Danes.

AD911 French give Normandy to the Vikings under King Rollo (Hrolf).

AD930 One of many meetings of the Iceland Althing. The settlement of Iceland is largely completed.

AD937 At the Battle of Brunanburh, Athelstan of Wessex defeats an alliance of Danes, Scots and Welsh.

AD940 Edmund of Wessex makes peace with Olaf of Jorvik.

AD875

AD900

AD925

AD95

Greenland Sea

GREENLAND

Norwegian Sea

NORWAY

SWEDEN

Thingvellir
ICELAND

Brattahlid

Birka

HEBRIDES

Kaupang

North Atlantic Ocean

SCOTLAND

Lindisfarne
priory is
burned

DENMARK

Ribe

Dublin

York
(Jorvik)

Hedeby

IRELAND

WALES

ENGLAND

FRANCE

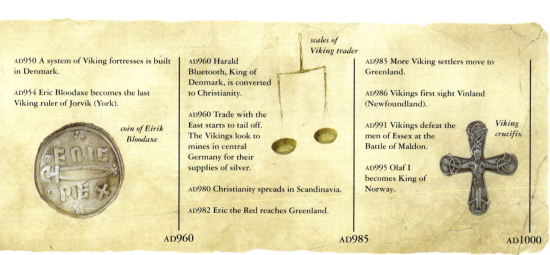

*scales of
Viking trader*

AD950 A system of Viking fortresses is built in Denmark.

AD954 Eric Bloodaxe becomes the last Viking ruler of Jorvik (York).

*coin of Eirik
Bloodaxe*

AD960 Harald Bluetooth, King of Denmark, is converted to Christianity.

AD960 Trade with the East starts to tail off. The Vikings look to mines in central Germany for their supplies of silver.

AD980 Christianity spreads in Scandinavia.

AD982 Eric the Red reaches Greenland.

AD985 More Viking settlers move to Greenland.

AD986 Vikings first sight Vinland (Newfoundland).

AD991 Vikings defeat the men of Essex at the Battle of Maldon.

AD995 Olaf I becomes King of Norway.

*Viking
crucifix*

AD960

AD985

AD1000

Viking Heroes

BRAVERY AND A SPIRIT OF ADVENTURE were greatly admired by the Vikings. The names and nicknames of their heroes – explorers, ruthless pirates and brave warriors – have gone down in history. Two of the most famous were Ragnar Hairy-Breeks, who terrorized the city of Paris in AD846, and a red-bearded Norwegian, called Eric the Red, who named and settled Greenland in AD985.

The Vikings we know most about were powerful kings. Harald Hardradi (meaning stern in counsel) saw his brother, King Olaf of Norway, killed in battle. He then fled to Russia and went on to join the emperor's bodyguard in Constantinople. After quarreling with the Empress Zoë, he returned to Russia before becoming ruler of Norway.

BLOODAXE
This coin is from Eric Bloodaxe's reign. He was the son of Norway's first king and ruled Jorvik (York).

Viking women could be just as tough and stubborn as their men. They were well respected, too. Archaeologists found two women buried in a splendid ship at Oseberg in Norway. One was a queen, the other her servant. They were buried with beautiful treasures.

MEMORIAL IN STONE
This memorial was raised at Jelling in Denmark by King Harald Bluetooth. An inscription on it says that King Harald "won all of Denmark and Norway and made all the Danes Christians."

FROM WARRIOR TO SAINT
Olaf Tryggvasön was Harald Finehair's grandson. He seized the throne of Norway in AD995. King Olaf became a Christian and was made a saint after his death in AD1000.

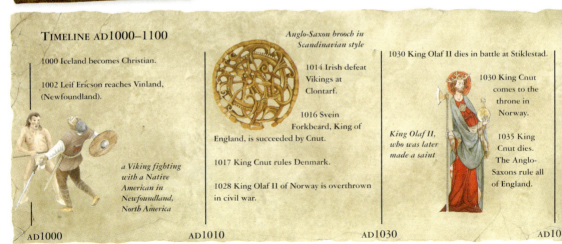

TIMELINE AD1000–1100

1000 Iceland becomes Christian.

1002 Leif Ericson reaches Vinland, (Newfoundland).

a Viking fighting with a Native American in Newfoundland, North America

Anglo-Saxon brooch in Scandinavian style

1014 Irish defeat Vikings at Clontarf.

1016 Svein Forkbeard, King of England, is succeeded by Cnut.

1017 King Cnut rules Denmark.

1028 King Olaf II of Norway is overthrown in civil war.

1030 King Olaf II dies in battle at Stiklestad.

1030 King Cnut comes to the throne in Norway.

King Olaf II, who was later made a saint

1035 King Cnut dies. The Anglo-Saxons rule all of England.

AD1000   AD1010   AD1030   AD10

THE NORMANS

Hrolf, or Rollo, was a Viking chief. In AD911 he and his followers were granted part of northern France by the French king. The region became known as Normandy, and the Normans went on to conquer Britain and parts of Italy.

THE WISE RULER

Cnut was the son of Svein Forkbeard, King of Denmark. He led extremely savage raids on England, becoming its king in 1016. He proved to be a kinder and wiser king than he had been a warrior. By 1018 he was King of Denmark and by 1030 he had become King of Norway as well. He died at Shaftesbury, England, in 1035.

LEIF THE LUCKY

Leif the Lucky was Eric the Red's son. He sailed even further west than his famous father. In about AD1000 he reached Canada, sailing to a land he named Vinland. This was probably Newfoundland. Other Vikings, including Leif's brother Thorwald, tried to settle these North American lands, but with little success.

Elizabeth, Russian wife of Harald Hardradi

1047 Harald Hardradi is made King of Norway.

1050 Oslo founded by Harald Hardradi.

1053 The Norman Empire begins in southern Italy.

1066 Harald Hardradi invades England. He is defeated by Harold I at the Battle of Stamford Bridge. An exhausted Harold I is in turn defeated by William of Normandy at the Battle of Hastings.

Norwegian foot soldier with ax

1070 The English pay Danegeld (a ransom) to persuade the Viking raiders to leave them alone.

1080 Cnut IV becomes King of Denmark.

1084 The Normans sack (raid) Rome.

1086 Cnut IV is assassinated.

1087 William of Normandy dies.

1098 King Magnus III of Norway asserts his authority over the Orkneys, the Hebrides and the Isle of Man. Although these were Viking settlements, there was dissent in these places.

1100 End of Viking era.

AD1070   AD1080   AD1100

Mesoamerican Civilizations

THE AZTECS LIVED IN MESOAMERICA – the region where North and South America meet. It includes the countries of Mexico, Guatemala, Honduras, El Salvador and Belize. During the past 3,000 years, Mesoamerica has been home to many great civilizations, including the Olmecs, the Maya, the Toltecs and the Aztecs. The Aztecs were the last of these to arrive, coming from the north in around AD1200. In about 1420 they began to conquer a mighty empire. However, in 1521 they were themselves conquered by Spanish soldiers, who came to America in search of gold. Over the next hundred years, the rest of Mesoamerica also fell to the Spaniards.

Even so, the descendants of these cultures still live in the area today. Many ancient Mesoamerican words, customs and beliefs survive, as do beautiful hand-painted books, mysterious ruins and amazing treasures.

OLMEC POWER

This giant stone head was carved by the Olmecs, the earliest of many great civilizations that flourished in Mesoamerica. Like the Maya and Aztecs, the Olmecs were skilled stoneworkers and built great cities.

UNCOVERING THE PAST

This temple is in Belize. Remains of such great buildings give archaeologists important clues about the people who built them.

TIMELINE 5000BC–AD800

Various civilizations were powerful in Mesoamerica at different times. The Maya were most successful between AD600–900. The Aztecs were at the height of their power from AD1428–AD1520.

Olmec figure

5000BC The Maya settle along the Pacific and Caribbean coasts of Mesoamerica.

2000BC People begin to farm in Belize, Guatemala and southeast Mexico.

2000BC The beginning of the period known as the Preclassic era.

1200BC Olmec people are powerful in Mesoamerica. They remain an important power until 400BC.

1000BC Maya craftworkers begin to copy Olmec pottery and jade carvings.

900BC Maya farmers design and use irrigation systems.

600BC The Zapotec civilization begins to flourish at Monte Alban.

Maya codex

300BC The Maya population starts to grow rapidly. Cities are built.

292BC The first-known Maya writing is produced.

150BC–AD500 The people living in the city of Teotihuacan grow powerful.

AD250 The beginning of the greatest period of Maya power, known as the Classic Maya era. This lasts until AD900.

mask from Teotihuac[]

5000BC   2000BC   300BC   AD5[]

THE GREAT TEMPLE

The Maya built this pyramid at Chichen-Itza in south-eastern Mexico, around AD1000. Historians believe that the Putun people may also have established themselves at Chichen-Itza. The pyramid was designed so that twice a year the Sun casts a snake-shaped shadow down the steps. Buildings like this tell us about the religious beliefs of the Maya and also show what skillful builders they were. Maya and Aztec stone masons worked without the help of metal tools.

THE FACE OF A GOD

This mask represents the god Tezcatlipoca. It is made of pieces of semiprecious stone fixed to a real human skull. Masks like this were worn during religious ceremonies, or displayed in temples as offerings to the gods.

MESSAGES IN CODE

These are Aztec picture-symbols for days, written in a folding book called a codex. Mesoamerican civilizations kept records of important people, places and events in picture-writing.

Home of the Mesoamerican civilizations

MESOAMERICA IN THE WORLD

For centuries, Mesoamerica was home to many different civilizations, but there were links between them, especially in farming, technology and religious beliefs. Until around AD1500, these Mesoamerican civilizations had very little contact with the rest of the world.

AD550 This is the time of the Maya's greatest artistic achievements. Fine temples and palaces in cities such as Kabah, Copan, Palenque, Uxmal and Tikal are built. These great regional city-states are ruled by lords who claim to be descended from the gods. This period of Maya success continues until AD900.

temple at Tikal

AD615 The great Maya leader Lord Pacal rules in the city of Palenque.

AD650 The city of Teotihuacan begins to decline. It is looted and burned by unknown invaders around AD700.

AD684 Lord Pacal's rule ends. He is buried in a tomb within the Temple of the Inscriptions in Palenque.

jade death mask of Lord Pacal

Bonampak mural

AD790 Splendid Maya wall-paintings are created in the royal palace in the city of Bonampak.

AD600   AD700   AD800

The Rise and Fall of Empires

MESOAMERICA IS A LAND of contrasts. There are high, jagged mountains, harsh deserts and swampy lakes. In the north, volcanoes rumble. In the south, dense, steamy forests have constant rain for half the year. These features made traveling around difficult, and also restricted contact between the regions.

Mesoamerica was never ruled as a single, united country. For centuries it was divided into separate states, each based on a city that ruled the surrounding countryside. Different groups of people and their cities became rich and strong in turn, before their civilizations weakened and faded away.

Historians divide the Mesoamerican past into three main periods. In Preclassic times (2000BC–AD250), the Olmecs were most powerful. The Classic era (AD250–900) saw the rise of the Maya and the people living in the city of Teotihuacan. During the Postclassic era (AD900–1500), the Toltecs, followed by the Aztecs, controlled the strongest states.

Each civilization had its own language, laws, traditions and skills, but there were also many links between the separate states. They all built big cities and organized long-distance trade. They all practiced human sacrifice and worshiped the same family of gods. And, unlike all other ancient American peoples, they all measured time using their own holy calendar of 260 days.

Sierra Madre Occidental

MEXICO

N

TIMELINE AD800–AD1400

AD800 The Maya palace-city of Palenque begins to decline.

AD856 The Toltecs of northern Mexico begin to create the city-state of Tula.

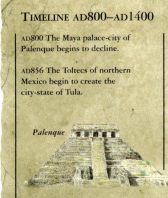
Palenque

AD900 Maya power begins to collapse. Many Maya cities, temples and palaces are deserted and overgrown by the rain forest. This is the beginning of the period known as the Post-classic era. The era lasts until AD1500.

AD950 The city of Tula becomes the center of fast-growing Toltec power.

AD986 According to legend, the Toltec god-king Quetzalcoatl leaves north Mexico for the Maya lands of Yucatan.

Toltec warrior

1000 The Maya city of Chichen-Itza becomes powerful. Historians believe that the Maya may have been helped by Putun warriors from the Gulf coast of Mexico.

1000 Toltec merchants do business along long-distance trade routes around the coast. They are helped by Maya craftworkers. Long-distance trade has already been taking place in Mesoamerica for hundreds of years.

1011–1063 The Mixtecs are ruled by the leader Eight Deer, in the area of Oaxaca. The Mixtecs are master goldsmiths.

AD800   AD900   AD1000   AD1100

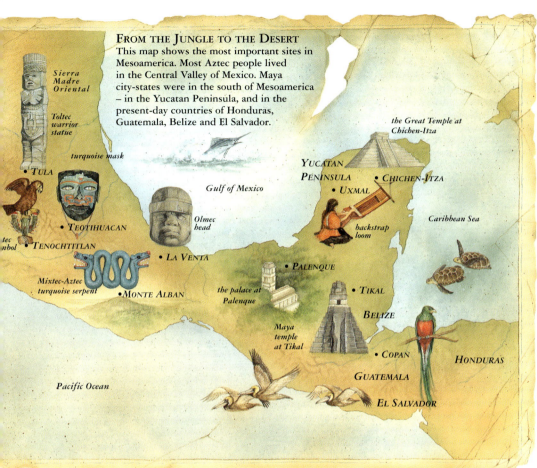

FROM THE JUNGLE TO THE DESERT

This map shows the most important sites in Mesoamerica. Most Aztec people lived in the Central Valley of Mexico. Maya city-states were in the south of Mesoamerica – in the Yucatan Peninsula, and in the present-day countries of Honduras, Guatemala, Belize and El Salvador.

Sierra Madre Oriental

Toltec warrior statue

turquoise mask

• **TULA**

tec mbol

• **TEOTIHUACAN**

• **TENOCHTITLAN**

Mixtec-Aztec turquoise serpent

• **MONTE ALBAN**

Gulf of Mexico

Olmec head

• **LA VENTA**

the palace at Palenque

• **PALENQUE**

Maya temple at Tikal

the Great Temple at Chichen-Itza

YUCATAN PENINSULA

• **CHICHEN-ITZA**

• **UXMAL**

backstrap loom

• **TIKAL**

BELIZE

Caribbean Sea

• **COPAN**

HONDURAS

GUATEMALA

EL SALVADOR

Pacific Ocean

1100 Aztecs leave their homeland in the dry, semidesert land to the north of Mexico and travel southward in search of a new place to live.

Aztec settlers

1168 The Chichimec people from central Mexico destroy the city of Tula and end Toltec power.

Aztec warrior

c.1200 Aztecs arrive in central Mexico. They find Tepanecs, Culhuas and Acolhuacans living there. At first, the Aztecs work as soldiers and slaves for these people, but they grow strong and fight against their masters.

c.1220 A new Maya city is founded at Mayapan.

1300 The Mixtec civilization begins to thrive in Oaxaca, southern Mexico.

1325 Aztecs found the city of Tenochtitlan on an island in the center of Lake Texcoco, central Mexico.

1350 Aztecs begin to build *chinampas* (gardens) around Lake Texcoco.

1372–91 The first-known Aztec ruler, Acamapichtli, reigns.

eagle on cactus, the symbol of Tenochtitlan

AD1200

AD1300

AD1400

Mesoamerican History Makers

FAME IN MAYA AND AZTEC times usually came with power. We know the names of powerful Aztec and Maya rulers, and sometimes of their wives. However, very few ordinary people's names have been discovered.

Rulers' names were written in a codex (book) or carved on a monument to record success in battle or other great achievements. Scribes also compiled family histories, in which rulers often claimed to be descended from gods. This gave them extra religious power. Aztec and Maya rulers made sure their names lived on by building huge palaces, amazing temples and tombs.

Some of the most well-known Mesoamerican rulers lived at a time when their civilization was under threat from outsiders. Explorers from Europe have left us detailed accounts and descriptions of the rulers they met.

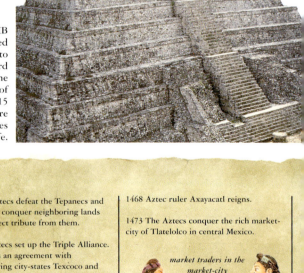

ROYAL TOMB
This pyramid-shaped temple was built to house the tomb of Lord Pacal. He ruled the Maya city-state of Palenque from AD615 to 684. Its walls are decorated with scenes from Pacal's life.

MAYA RULER
This statue shows a ruler from the Maya city of Kabah, in Mexico. Most Maya statues were designed as symbols of power, rather than as lifelike portraits.

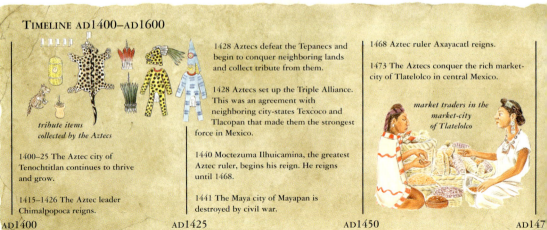

TIMELINE AD1400–AD1600

tribute items collected by the Aztecs

1400–25 The Aztec city of Tenochtitlan continues to thrive and grow.

1415–1426 The Aztec leader Chimalpopoca reigns.

1428 Aztecs defeat the Tepanecs and begin to conquer neighboring lands and collect tribute from them.

1428 Aztecs set up the Triple Alliance. This was an agreement with neighboring city-states Texcoco and Tlacopan that made them the strongest force in Mexico.

1440 Moctezuma Ilhuicamina, the greatest Aztec ruler, begins his reign. He reigns until 1468.

1441 The Maya city of Mayapan is destroyed by civil war.

1468 Aztec ruler Axayacatl reigns.

1473 The Aztecs conquer the rich market-city of Tlatelolco in central Mexico.

market traders in the market-city of Tlatelolco

AD1400   AD1425   AD1450   AD147

GOLD-SEEKER

Soldier and explorer Hernando Cortés (1485–1547) came from a poor but noble Spanish family. After Columbus' voyages, many Spanish adventurers traveled to Mesoamerica and the Caribbean hoping to make their fortunes. Cortés sailed to Cuba and then, in 1519, went on to explore Mexico. His example inspired many treasure-seekers. One such man, Pizarro, went on to conquer the Incas of Peru.

THE LAST EMPEROR

Aztec emperor Moctezuma II (above right) ruled from 1502 to 1520. He was the last emperor to control the Aztec lands. Moctezuma II was a powerful warrior and a good administrator, but he was tormented by gloomy prophecies and visions of disaster. He was captured when Cortés and his soldiers invaded the capital city of Tenochtitlan in 1519. The following year he was stoned in a riot while trying to plead with his own people.

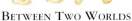

BETWEEN TWO WORLDS

Malintzin (far right above) was from a Mesoamerican state hostile to the Aztecs. She was of vital help to the Spanish conquerors because she spoke the Aztec language and quickly learned Spanish. The Spanish called her Doña Marina.

1481–1486 Aztec ruler Tizoc reigns.

1486 Aztec ruler Ahuitzotl begins his reign.

1487 The Aztecs' Great Temple in Tenochtitlan is finished. Twenty thousand captives are sacrificed at a special ceremony to consecrate it (make it holy).

1492 The European explorer Christopher Columbus sails across the Atlantic Ocean to America.

Columbus lands

1502 Columbus sails along the coast of Mesoamerica and meets Maya people.

a comet appears in the sky

1502–1520 Moctezuma II reigns. During his reign, a comet appears in the sky. Aztec astronomers fear that this, and other strange signs, mean the end of the world.

1519 Hernan Cortés, a Spanish soldier, arrives in Mexico. A year later, Cortés and his soldiers attack Tenochtitlan. Moctezuma II is killed.

1521 The Spanish destroy Tenochtitlan.

1525 Spain takes control of Aztec lands.

1527 Maya lands are invaded by the Spanish.

1535 Mexico becomes a Spanish colony.

1600 War and European diseases wipe out 10 million Aztecs, leaving fewer than a million, but the Aztec language and many customs live on. By 1600, between 75% and 90% of Maya people are also dead, but their skills, beliefs and traditions survive.

Spanish soldier

AD1500   AD1525   AD1600

The First North Americans

DESCENDANTS OF THE ANASAZIS, who were among the earliest known North American Indians, have colorful tales of their origins. One story tells how their ancestors climbed into the world through a hole. Another describes how all of the tribes were created from a fierce monster who was ripped apart by a brave coyote. The early history of the many nations or tribes is not clear, though archaeological finds have helped to build a picture of their way of life. If you could step back to before 1500, you would find that the United States and Canada were home to hundreds of different Indian tribes. Each had its own leader(s) and a distinctive language and culture. Some tribes were nomadic, some settled permanently in large communities. Remains of pottery, woodcarvings and jewelry show how many of the North American peoples developed expert craft skills.

KEEPING THE PAST ALIVE

Descendants of the different tribes survive throughout North America, passing down stories and traditions to new generations. This boy in Wyoming is dressed in ceremonial costume for a modern powwow. He is helping to preserve his tribe's cultural history.

BRIDGING THE GAP

Archaeological evidence suggests that the first American Indians traveled from Asia. They crossed ice and land bridges formed at the Bering Strait around 13,000BC or earlier. From here, they moved south, some settling along the coasts.

TIMELINE 32,000BC–AD1400

Most historians believe that hunters walked to North America from Siberia. Evidence suggests there may have been two migrations – one around 32,000BC, the second between 28,000BC and 13,000BC. Some historians think there may have been earlier ancient populations already living there. More research is needed to support this theory. The hunters spread out, each group, or tribe, adapting their way of life to suit their environment. Later, some gave up the nomadic hunting life and began to settle as farmers.

3000BC Inuit of the Arctic are probably the last settlers to come from Asia.

1000BC Early cultures are mound builders such as the Adena and later, the Hopewell people. The Hopewell are named after the farmer on whose Ohio land their main site was found.

1000BC Farming cultures develop in the Southwest with agricultural skills brought in from Mexico.

serpent mound of the Hopewell culture

black and yellow maize

300BC–AD1450 Cultures, such as the Hohokam, use shells as currency.

AD200 (or before) There is evidence of corn being grown by the mound-building people, probably introduced from Mexico.

AD700–900 Pueblo people bury their dead with black and white painted pots.

3000BC

300BC

burial pot

FALSE FACE

Dramatic, carved masks were worn by several tribes to ward off evil spirits thought to cause illnesses. This one is from the Iroquois people. It was known as a False Face mask because it shows an imaginary face. False Face ceremonies are still performed in North America today.

BUCKSKIN RECORD

Tales of events were painted on animal skins, such as this one, created by an Apache. The skins serve as a form of history book. North American Indians had no real written alphabet, so much of the evidence about their way of life comes from pictures.

DIGGING UP EVIDENCE

Hopewell Indians made this bird from hammered copper. It dates back to around 300BC and was uncovered in a burial mound in Ohio. The mounds were full of intricate trinkets buried alongside the dead. Finds like this tell us about the crafts, materials and customs of the time.

ANCIENT TOWN

Acoma (right) is one of the oldest continuously inhabited traditional Pueblo settlements in the Southwest. It is still partly inhabited by Pueblo descendants. The Pueblo people were given their name by Spaniards who arrived in the area in 1540. *Pueblo* is a Spanish word meaning village. It was used to describe the kind of tribe that lived in a cluster of houses built from mud and stone. Flat-roofed homes were built in terraces, two or three stories high.

AD700 Mound-building cultures build temples at Cahokia near the Mississippi. The city holds the largest population in North America before the 1800s.

AD900 Earliest Anasazis (ancient people) on the Colorado Plateau live in sunken-pit homes. Later they build their homes above the ground but keep pit dwellings as kivas, which are their religious buildings.

kiva (underground temple) of the Anasazis

AD982 First Europeans reach Greenland (northeast of Canada) under the Viking, Eric the Red.

1002 Leif Ericson lands in Newfoundland, Canada, and creates the first European settlements. *Vikings arrive*

1100 The Anasazi people move into the mountains, building settlements in cliffs.

Mesa Verde, a cliff palace

1200 The Calusa in Florida are skillful carvers and craftsmen who trade extensively.

1270s–1300 Anasazis abandon many of their prehistoric sites and stone cities – many move eastward.

1300 Beginnings of the Pueblo tribes (Hopi and Zuni) in the Southwest. Many of these are descendants of the Anasazis.

AD1400

Inhabiting a Vast Land

orca
(killer whale)

THE FIRST NORTH AMERICANS were hunters who followed musk oxen, buffaloes and other animals to the grassland interior of the huge continent. Early settlements grew up in the rugged, hostile terrain of the Southwest where three dominant cultures evolved. The Mogollon (Mountain People) are thought to be the first Southwest dwellers to build houses, make pottery and grow their own food from around 300BC. The Hohokam (Vanished Ones) devised an extensive canal system to irrigate the desert as early as 100BC, while the Anasazi (Ancient Ones) were basketmakers who built their homes high among the cliffs and canyons.

In contrast, the eastern and midwestern lands abounded with plant and animal life. Here, tribes such as the Adena (1000BC to AD200) and the Hopewell (300BC to AD700), created huge earth mounds to bury their dead. The central Great Plains was home to over 30 different tribes, who lived by hunting buffalo. In the far north, the Inuit had a similar existence, relying on caribou and seals for their food and clothes. Europeans began to arrive around AD982 with the Vikings. Then in the 1500s, Spanish explorers came looking for gold, land and slaves. Over the next 400 years, many other foreign powers laid claim to different parts of the land. By 1910, the native population was at its lowest, about 400,000, and many tribes had been forced from their homelands onto reservations.

TRIBAL HOMELANDS

In the 1400s, there were more than 300 tribes, or nations, spread across North America (between two and three million people). These are often divided into ten cultural areas based on the local environment:

1 Arctic
2 Subarctic
3 Woodlands
4 Southeast
5 Great Plains
6 Southwest
7 Great Basin
8 Plateau
9 Northwest Coast
10 California

TIMELINE AD1400–1780

1400 Apaches arrive in the Southwest, probably by two routes – one from the Plains after following migrating buffaloes, the other via the Rockies.

1492 Christopher Columbus sails from Spain to the Bahamas where he meets the peaceful, farming Arawaks.

1510 The powerful Calusas of Florida abandon their ancient center, Key Marco, possibly after hearing of foreign invaders.

1513 Calusas drive off Ponce de León, a Spanish explorer.

Columbus

1541 Zuni people get a first glimpse of horses when Spain's Francisco Vasquez de Coronado travels to the Southwest.

1541 Caddo people of the Plains oppose Spanish Hernando de Soto's soldiers.

1542 The large Arawak population that Columbus first encountered has been reduced to just 200 people. Ten years later the Arawaks die out through mistreatment.

shell wampum belt celebrates the League of Five Nations

1550 League of Five Nations is formed by the Seneca, Cayuga, Mohawk, Oneida and Onondaga tribes in the Northeast to create a strong government. They are referred to as the Iroquois.

1585 Sir Walter Raleigh reaches the northeast coast and, ignoring the rights of the Secotan natives, claims the land for the English, calling it Virginia.

1590 Raleigh and John White return to Virginia, but the colony has disappeared. White draws pictures documenting Secotan life.

AD1400   AD1540   AD1550   AD159

BAFFIN ISLAND

seal

NEWFOUNDLAND

1

Inuit with igloo

Hudson Bay

Inuit fisherman

2

QUEBEC

Chipewyan canoe

Cree

Cree

Tsimshian

Plains Cree

2

Algonquin

Blackfoot   Hidatsa

Ojibwa

Huron

9

Plains Ojibwa

beaver

8   salmon   Mandan

3   New York

Nootka   Crow   corn

Chippewa   Iroquois

Nez Perce   Western Sioux   Menominee   Algonquian groups

Shoshone   Pawnee   Sioux   Washington

Salish   Arapaho   Powhatan

7   Ute   N

Washoe   Cheyenne warrior   hunting buffaloes

Cayuse   Secotan village

Yurok   Osage

10   Paiute basket-make   Hopi katchina doll

Hopewell mound

Chumash   Navajo hogans   Kiowa camp   Wichita   Cherokee village of Echota

Los Angeles   Mohave   NEW MEXICO   Apache   Comanche   Chickasaw   Creek   eagle

Choctaw   Seminole

6   Pueblo village   TEXAS   Natchez   Calusa   Miami

salmon

1598 Juan de Onate founds the first Spanish colony on Pueblo Indian land.

1600s Shoshone acquire horses from the South-west (brought there by Spanish invaders) and they spread across the Great Plains.

horses on the Plains

1607 Jamestown colony is founded on Powhatan land.

1607 Pamunkey members of the Powhatan Confederacy take John Smith prisoner.

1620 The Mayflower Pilgrims arrive on the East Coast and are helped by the Wampanoag.

1650 Guns from European traders (at first flintlocks, later rifles) begin to take the place of traditional weapons.

1707 A Russian expedition reaches North-west Coast to discover that it is inhabited.

willow bow

rifle

coup stick

1722 League of Five Nations increases to six when the Tuscarora join the group.

1750 Sioux tribes move to the Plains.

1774 Juan Perez sails to the North-west Coast and takes it for Spain. European diseases almost wipe out the Haida people.

1771 Five missions are set up on Chumash land, California, to try to convert North Americans to Christianity (this leads to a revolt in 1824).

AD1620   AD1710   Haida totem pole

Shapers of History

MANY NORTH AMERICAN Indians who have earned a place in history lived around the time that Europeans reached North America. They became famous for their dealings with explorers and with the white settlers who were trying to reorganize the lives of Indian nations. Some tribes welcomed the new settlers. Others tried to negotiate peacefully for rights to their own land. Those who led their people in battles, against the settlers, became the most legendary. One of these was Geronimo, who led the last defiant group of Chiricahua Apaches in their fight to preserve the tribe's homeland and culture.

POCAHONTAS (1595–1617)
The princess became a legend, and the topic of a Disney film, for protecting English Captain John Smith against her father, Chief Powhatan. The English took Pocahontas captive to force Powhatan's people to agree to their demands. She married John Rolfe, an English soldier, and in 1616 left for England with their baby. She never returned, as she died of smallpox, in Gravesend, Kent, aged 22.

CORNPLANTER (died 1796)
In the 1700s, Cornplanter was a chief of the Iroquois. He was a friend to the colonists and fought on their side in the Revolution of 1776–85. The land of Cornplanter's tribe was spoiled but his people were given a reservation for their help. Many Iroquois people fought on the side of the British which split the group.

Opechancanough, Powhatan

Black Hawk, Sauk

Geronimo, Apache

Pontiac, Ottawa

Lapowinsa, Lenape

TIMELINE AD1780–1924

1783 The colonists (settlers) sign a treaty with Britian which recognizes their independence and calls them Americans. The tribes are never regarded as American.

1788 The Chinook in the Northwest have their first encounter with Europeans when they meet Englishman John Mears.

1789 Explorers encounter Kutchin and other Subarctic tribes, who later set up trade with the Hudson's Bay Company (formed in 1831).

1795 Tecumseh refuses to sign the Treaty of Greenville giving up Shawnee land.

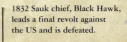

William Clark and Meriwether Lewis

1803 The US federal government buys Mississippi land from the French, squeezing out the Indians even more.

1804 Sacajawea guides Lewis and Clark on the first overland journey from Mississippi to the Pacific Coast.

1830–40s Painters such as Frederic Remington, George Catlin and Karl Bodmer, document lifestyles of the Plains Indians.

1832 Sauk chief, Black Hawk, leads a final revolt against the US and is defeated.

1848 Discovery of gold in California.

coming the tra[...]

1848–58 Palouse tribe of the Plateau resist white domination, refusing to join a reservation.

George Catlin painting a Mandan chief

AD1780   AD1803   AD1848

SARAH WINNEMUCCA (1844–1891)

Sarah was from the Paviotso Paiutes of northern Nevada. Her grandfather escorted British Captain John Frémont in his exploration of the West in the 1840s. But in 1860 her mother, sister and brother were all killed in the Paiute War against white settlers. Sarah acted as a mediator between her people and the settlers to help improve conditions. She later wrote a book, *Life Among the Paiutes*, telling of the tribe's suffering and her own life.

SITTING BULL (1831–1890)

The Hunkpapa Sioux had a spiritual leader, a medicine man known as Sitting Bull. He brought together subtribes of the Sioux and refused to sign treaties giving up the sacred Black Hills in South Dakota. He helped to defeat General Custer at Little Bighorn.

TECUMSEH (died 1813)

A great chief of the Shawnees, Tecumseh, tried to unite tribes of the Mississippi valley, Old Northwest and South against the United States. He even fought for the British against the US in the 1812–14 war. The picture shows his death.

Oscelo, Seminole

Red Cloud, Sioux

Chief Joseph

PROTECTING THEIR TRIBES

These eight North American chiefs are some of the most famous. Not all fought. Lapowinsa of Delaware, was cheated out of land when he signed a contract allowing settlers as much land as they could cover in a day and a half. Pontiac traded with the French but despised English intrusion. Chief Joseph tried to negotiate peacefully for land for the Nez Percé tribe but died in exile. Red Cloud successfully fought to stop gold seekers invading Sioux hunting grounds.

1850 The Navajo sign their third treaty with the US but hostilities continue.

1850s–80s Railroads open up the West to settlers.

1864 The Long Walk – Navajo people and animals are massacred by US troops, their homes burned. Survivors are forced to walk over 300 miles to Fort Sumner.

1864 Sand Creek Massacre – 300 Cheyenne women and children are killed by US soldiers.

1876 General Custer is killed by Sioux warriors in the Battle of Little Bighorn.

1886 Surrender of Geronimo to the US. He is a prisoner for many years.

Sand Creek Massacre

1890 Ghost dance springs up as Sioux tribes mourn their dead – it worries the white settlers who see it as provocation.

1890 Sitting Bull is killed at Standing Rock (a Sioux reservation) by Indian police hired by the US.

1890 Sioux chief Big Foot and many of his tribe are killed in the Massacre of Wounded Knee. This ends the Sioux's struggle for their homelands.

buffalo coin

1924 US citizenship granted to American Indians and marked by a coin bearing a buffalo.

AD1870

ghost dance shirt

AD1924

Glossary

A

alabaster A white stone used for making ornaments.

alloy A mixture of metals melted together to create a new metal that may be stronger or easier to work.

Althing An assembly of free men that passed laws in Iceland at the time of the Vikings.

amphitheater A large, oval open-air arena surrounded by seats, used for public shows such as gladiator fights.

Anno Domini (AD) A system used to calculate dates after the supposed year of Christ's birth. Anno Domini dates in this book are prefixed AD up to the year 1000 (e.g. AD521). After 1000 no prefixes are used (e.g. 1429).

aqueduct A channel for carrying water over long distances.

archaeology The scientific study of the past looking at things people have left behind, such as tools or jewelry.

astrology The belief that stars, planets and other heavenly bodies shape our lives.

astronomy The scientific study of stars, planets, comets and other heavenly bodies.

B

barter The exchange of goods, one for the other.

Before Christ (BC) The system used to calculate dates before the supposed year of Christ's birth. Dates are claculated in reverse (e.g. 2,000BC is longer ago than 200BC).

Brahman A high-status Hindu, often a priest.

bronze A metal alloy, made by mixing copper with tin.

C

campaign A series of battles fought by a ruler to bring an area under his control.

cartouche The oval border used in Egyptian hieroglyphics to show that the name it contains is a pharoah or a god.

circa (c.) Approximately. The symbol *c.* is used when the exact date of something is not known.

citizen A free person belonging to a city, country or empire. Only citizens had full rights such as the right to vote.

city-state A city and the area surrounding it which is controlled by one leader or government.

civilization A settled society that makes advances in the arts, sciences, law or government.

clan A group of people related to each other by ancestry or marriage.

consul One of two leaders of the Roman republic elected each year.

cuneiform The first system of writing. It was invented by the Sumerians of Mesopotamia.

cylinder seal A small carved stone with a raised or sunken pattern. It could be rolled across soft clay to leave an impression. Seals identified the goods belonging to a person.

D

Daoism A Chinese philosophy based on contemplation of the natural world.

dynasty A royal family, or the time it remains in power.

E

edict An order from a ruler or a government.

empire A large number of different lands ruled over by a single person or government.

evolution The changes that take place in an animal or plant species over millions of years, as it becomes more complex.

excavation A place where archaeologists are digging up the ground in order to discover more about the past.

F

flax A plant which yields fibers that can be woven into cloth.

G

geometry A branch of mathematics concerning the measurements of lines, angles and surfaces.

H

hieroglyphic A picture symbol used in writing.

human sacrifice Killing people as an offering to the gods.

hunter-gatherer A person whose way of life involves hunting wild animals and gathering plant foods.

I

imperial Relating to the rule of an emperor or empress.

inscribed Lettering, pictures or patterns carved into stone or wood.

irrigate To bring water to dry land in order to grow crops.

ivory The hard, smooth, cream-colored part of the tusks of elephants and walruses.

J

jade A very hard, smooth, green stone. Jade was highly prized in China and Mesoamerica.

K

kaolin A fine white clay used in porcelain and papermaking.
kiln Industrial oven in which clay or enamel, for example, are fired.

L

limestone A type of rock often used in building.
loom A frame or machine used for weaving cloth.
lyre A harp-like musical instrument.

M

Mayflower **Pilgrims** The first European settlers in North America.
Mesopotamia The fertile region between the Tigris and Euphrates rivers, where the world's first cities grew up.
Minotaur A mythical beast, half man half bull, that was said by the ancient Greeks to live in Crete.
mosaic A craft in which tiny pieces of colorful stone, shell or glass are pieced together to make a design or picture to decorate floors, walls, tables and smaller objects.

N

Nawab A Muslim leader in India.
Near East The countries of the eastern Mediterranean, including Turkey, Egypt and Romania.
nomad A member of a group that roams from place to place to find food or to follow herds.

O

obelisk A pointed pillar, erected as a monument.

P

papyrus A tall reed that is used to make a kind of paper.
Parthenon A temple in Athens.
pestle A club-shaped tool for crushing seeds or grains.
pewter An alloy or mixture of metals, made from tin and lead.
philosophy A Greek word meaning love of knowledge. Philosophy is the discipline of thinking about the meaning of life.
pigment Any coloring used to make paint.
porcelain The finest quality of pottery. It was made with kaolin and baked at a high temperature.
prehistoric Belonging to the time before written records were made.
pyramid A large pointed monument with a broad, square base and pointed sides.

R

radiocarbon dating A very accurate method of dating objects.
relief A sculpture in which a design is carved from a flat surface, such as a wall.
ritual A traditional ceremony that is often religious.

S

Senate The law-making assembly of ancient Rome.
sickle A tool with a curved blade used to cut grass or grain crops.
Silk Road The overland trading route from China through to Europe.

sphinx The statue of a mythical creature, half human half lion.
stela A tall stone pillar.
sultanate The area controlled by a Muslim leader.
symbol A mark in a painting or on a stone, that has a special meaning.

T

tapestry A cloth with a design sewn onto it.
terra cotta A composition of baked clay and sand used to make statues and pottery.
textile Any cloth that has been woven, such as silk or cotton.
Thing An assembly of free men that passed laws in Viking lands.
tomb A vault in which dead bodies are placed.
travois A platform for baggage formed by poles roped together. It was dragged by a person or tied to the back of a dog or horse.
tribe A group of people that shared a common language and way of life.
turquoise A valuable stone that ranges in color from light blue to blue-green.

V

Venus figurine A small statue of a woman. She is usually shown with large hips, breasts and buttocks, and a full stomach. The figurines may have been worshipped as symbols of fertility or plenty, or carried as good luck charms.

Z

ziggurat A large Mesopotamian temple with a broad, square base and stepped sides.

Index

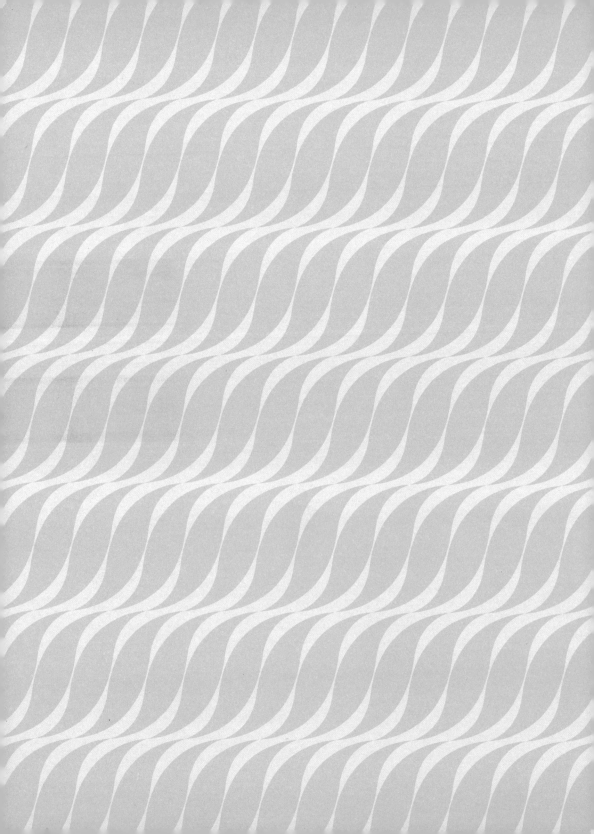